PRAGUE TRAVEL TIPS: An American's Guide to Her Adopted City

Krysti Brice

DEDICATION

This book is dedicated to my father, who encouraged me to write it.

CONTENTS

ACKNOWLEDGMENTS

My heartfelt gratitude goes to all those who helped me in various ways to create this book, especially: Iva, Stephanie, Janice, Claire, Amelia, Julia, Marshall, Angie, Millie, Colleen, Charlotte and Kim.

1 INTRODUCTION

Welcome to Prague, arguably one of the most beautiful cities in the world. It is certainly one of the most historic and well-preserved, and a visit here will take you back through layers of time, expressed through its architecture – from Romanesque to Gothic, Renaissance, Baroque and Rococo. And it doesn't stop there: you can continue to follow the footsteps of history to neo-Classical, neo-Gothic and neo-Renaissance, right through to Art Nouveau, Cubist, Modernist and Functionalist. And yes, if you really must, you can find a few communist-era structures as well. But in addition to the historic, you can also witness the ongoing rebirth of this city as expressed through a magnificent display of the particularly Central European art of blending the old and the new, the ancient and the ultra-modern, hip and trendy.

I have lived and worked in Prague for most of the past two decades, first as a financial advisor and now as a semi-retired writer, mentor and tour guide. The city that exists today is not the one I came to in February 1992. It has been experiencing a transformation that is still unfolding, in all areas of life – architecture, cuisine, culture, you name it. Sometimes, this act of finding its way can make Prague seem quite chaotic, especially for a visitor. In my work as a private tour guide, I have had the pleasure of leading people through this maze of history and change for almost a decade now. And as an American expatriate who has lived and worked here for many years, I have a unique perspective on life in Prague and the Czech Republic.

As part of my tour services, I began preparing customized "Tip Sheets" for each of my clients prior to their visits. These "Tip Sheets" answered frequently asked questions about practical matters and also helped my clients plan their evenings out and other activities while in Prague. It started as a kind of insider's guide to eating and shopping where those of us who live here do the same, listing the favorite haunts of other expats and discerning locals alike. Some years ago, I shared this Tip Sheet with my father, and his response was: "This guide is so good, you ought to publish it!" So, I did just that.

Those early tip sheets were greatly expanded since I first began preparing them, and eventually resulted in this book. However, please note that this is not a typical guidebook – you can get all the history and museum opening times you need from plenty of existing sources. Rather, it is your insider's guide to making your trip to Prague truly unique and local, and the practical information it contains is intended to help you with the things that can be baffling to visitors, given the difficulty of the language and the, unfortunately, still-all-too-common lack of a good attitude toward customer service.

I hope my book helps make your stay a breeze, and I wish you a great time in Prague! And if you think you'd like to take a private tour with me, please contact me through my website at www.exclusivepraguetours.com or email me at krysti.brice@seznam.cz.

2 ABOUT THIS BOOK

Thanks for buying my book! It is designed to give you a head start on your visit. It also provides restaurant, shopping and sightseeing suggestions; a few practical tips; and some words of caution about things like pickpockets and dishonest taxi drivers. I hope it will add some fun and convenience to your stay, as the knowledge I've gained while living here for almost two decades can save you time and energy to spend on sightseeing and enjoying Prague's beauty and atmosphere.

In addition to practical advice, this book is full of many of the things I love in Prague. The listings included here, like restaurants and galleries, are the places I (and many of my friends) like a lot and visit often. **So the recommendations and suggestions in this book are based on personal experience – almost nothing contained here (there are a few rare exceptions) is based on second-hand knowledge or recommendations from others.** I receive no commissions from any restaurants (thought I ought to, given the numbers of customers I've sent to many of them!). And in most cases, I have visited these restaurants and galleries at least once within the past year (or in some cases within an even more recent time period), some of them more than once.

However, please note that things change quickly in Prague, and information is not always forthcoming. Given the volume of tourist traffic and the nature of the local economy, which is still in a learning curve, businesses open and close quickly and often, only to be replaced by the next café or crystal shop.

A good example is a Czech pub in the center of town that I had listed in the first version of this book. You will note in the section below on "Czech Fare" that there aren't many such traditional pubs remaining in the center of town these days. With their cheaper pub prices, how could they survive? They've all been replaced by pricier chic restaurants (which are also great and are a welcome addition) and by larger pub chains that can afford the rents in Old Town. On a tour I gave not long after the book was published, I pointed out the pub in question to my clients. It was full of customers, as usual. But just two weeks later I was surprised to find on a walk through town that it was gone without a trace. There was no sign on the door, and the interior had already been stripped way. I had eaten there not too long before.

On the same walk through town, I learned that, sadly, one of the English language bookstores I recommended had closed as well. It had been in existence for a decade or more. As with the pub, no trace of the bookshop could be found, and I had also visited it about two weeks prior on the same tour with the clients to whom I had shown the restaurant! But as I said, information is not very forthcoming here – this is the land of Kafka, after all. I have since removed both listings from the book, but not before one reader had tried to dine at the pub in question and mentioned in his Amazon review that it was closed.

For the most part, though, the listings here are old standbys that have stood the test of time and that I have visited recently. All of the information is up to date as of this writing (March 2017), including the tram stops. Be aware, however, that the tram system recently underwent a huge reorganization, and for the first time in probably two decades, many of the tram routes have changed or have been cancelled. For this version of the book, I have checked all tram stops against the public transport website (and against my own knowledge and experience). However, I did notice that some of the **listings' individual websites** have **not** yet been updated to reflect the recent tram route changes and still provide the former (now invalid) tram numbers for reaching their locations. So, when using a particular listing's website for public transport connections, you might want to double check it against the public transport website (**www.dpp.cz/en**) or the information contained in this book.

And finally, tram networks, it seems, need to be incessantly dug up and re-laid every three or four years, and so it's almost inevitable that a particular tram will not be going where it usually goes at some time or another. To make things worse, this usually happens in the warm summer months, when most visitors like you will be here for your summer holidays! And, nothing about the changes will be provided in English. It will be posted at tram stops in long paragraphs of unusually and unnecessarily complicated Czech that even the Czechs have difficulty deciphering (evidenced by the fact that large numbers of them will be standing around for long periods of time staring at the posted information with blank or quizzical looks on their faces). So, if you don't see your desired tram number listed at a stop where it should be, or if you get on a tram and it takes you somewhere other than where you were intending to go, my advice is to ask somebody for help.

3 A BIT OF PRAGUE HISTORY

As stated in the introduction, this is not a typical guidebook, as my aim was to: share with you things that are **not** already in typical guidebooks; give you a local experience; help you sort through the millions of restaurant choices offered by sources like Trip Advisor®; and give you a practical "do this; don't do that" guide based on having figured out lots of confusing things after living here for many years. So, originally I hadn't included any historical information about Prague in this book, as my assumption was that you already have a traditional guidebook or otherwise know some basics about Prague and its history. I saw no point in reinventing the wheel, and that's also why this book doesn't list every Prague historical site or every art gallery and museum. Rather, it's a local's take on her (and other locals') favorite places to eat, things to do and places to see.

However, in an online review, one reader mentioned the lack of history as a drawback, and I figured he might have a point. So I decided to include some **very basic** historical information here. Prague is an ancient, beautiful and significant city. Its many centuries are rich and complex beyond measure. To include all of the details here would turn this book into a tome and would detract from my original purpose in writing it. And although I've completed a lot of both formal and informal study on Prague's history, especially its art history, I am not a historian. So if I were to do its history justice, I would simply be compiling information gathered from other sources. What I've done here is provide you with a quick take, in a nutshell, to give you some background to the tips that follow it.

Some Basic Facts

Prague (Praha in Czech), the capital of the Czech Republic, is also the capital of the lands historically known as Bohemia ("Čechy" in Czech). Located on the Vltava (or Moldau) River, Prague has a population of about 1.3 million (if you include the extended suburbs, the population is estimated to be around 2 million).

At various points in history, Prague has been a political, cultural, and economic center of Central Europe, with changing (and often tragic) fortunes and degrees of importance. Its central location has been both a blessing and a curse. Founded some 1,100 years ago during the Romanesque period, Prague has since that time had several standout centuries during which it has flourished – architecturally, culturally, intellectually and financially.

A History of Beauty

Chances are you're planning a trip to Prague because it is incredibly, magically beautiful. In reality, that's probably the main reason we visit most of the places we do, and in Prague's case, its beauty is over-the-top. And this beauty is a result largely, but not only, of a confluence of factors during those standout centuries I mentioned above.

Two of these periods were the Gothic and Renaissance, during the reigns of King Charles IV (14th century) and

Emperor Rudolf II (16th century), respectively. During their respective reigns, Prague was not only the capital of the Czech lands, but was also the capital of the Holy Roman Empire. That meant that a lot of wealth and political and religious power were concentrated here during those times, and Prague, quite simply, grew in importance – and its art and architecture flourished.

High Gothic

While much of Prague's Renaissance architecture did not stand the test of time, King Charles put a Gothic stamp on the city that gives it a special look and feel to this day. Most of the Gothic architecture you'll see is from King Charles' reign, and many of the city's most significant landmarks, such as St. Vitus Cathedral and the Charles Bridge with its Old Town bridge tower, were commissioned by Charles and designed by his chief architect, the talented Peter Parler. Many later Gothic structures, such as the Powder Tower were modeled on Parler's designs.

Even before Charles' reign, Prague's wealth began to grow after silver was discovered in the mountains of nearby Kutná Hora (see "Day Trips"). With the silver they extracted over several centuries, the local authorities began minting the Bohemian groschen, which became a very valuable and desired currency throughout Europe in the Middle Ages – the euro of its day. The town of Kutná Hora itself boomed and became very wealthy, and its Gothic architecture is some of the most stunning you'll see anywhere. Then in 14th-century Prague, Charles' stature as Holy Roman Emperor, combined with the continued circulation of the Bohemian groschen, fostered the blossoming of the capital's remarkable Gothic architecture.

Rudolf's Renaissance

In the 16th century, with the Czech lands under the control of the Hapsburgs, Austrian Emperor Rudolf II moved the capital of the empire to Prague, and he moved himself from Vienna and into Prague Castle. Rudolf has been described politely as being rather eccentric, and he also had a great love of art, music, alchemy, astronomy and more. The word around Europe at the time was that this "crazy" king was doling out lots of his money to satisfy his passions, so many artists and artisans, musicians and alchemists, including the astronomers Tycho Brahe and Johannes Kepler, flocked to Prague in order to take advantage of Rudolf's patronage.

The result was a beautiful Renaissance remodeling of Prague's Malá Strana district (most of which is lost now), fabulous artwork (located in Prague and throughout Europe) and a settlement of Italian artisans in an area of Malá Strana that later became known as the Italian Quarter. These artisans then passed their crafts on to their descendants who later fit the bill perfectly when the Baroque Counter-Reformation building boom began in the 17th century.

Defeat at White Mountain

The sheer volume, beauty and extravagance of the Baroque architecture and sculpture you'll see in Prague and other Czech towns is due largely to the Counter-Reformation building boom that began after the Battle of White Mountain which took place in 1620 during the Thirty Years' War. After mounting many resistance movements over several centuries against their Catholic rulers (who were seen as "occupiers"), Czech Protestant forces were roundly defeated at this battle, one that sealed victory in Bohemia for the Hapsburg's Catholic armies. After the Battle of White Mountain, the Hapsburgs would rule here for another four centuries uninterrupted.

To this day, Czechs speak of this definitive battle often and with a great sense of loss, mentioning it in everyday conversation as if it happened yesterday. Their lament is evident and is akin to the way some American Southerners speak of the Civil War in the United States: there is the sense that it was an event which sealed their fate and from which they never fully recovered.

Baroque Drama

With the Czech Protestant forces defeated and all thoughts of Protestant uprisings and reformations put to bed, the Counter-Reformation began in earnest. But by this time, the independent-minded Czechs, influenced two centuries earlier by Protestant reformer and national hero Jan Hus (who predated Martin Luther by a century), were very resistant to **any** kind of religion, especially Catholicism, which they viewed as the religion of "occupiers."

And precisely because the Czechs were so resistant to religion in general – and to Catholicism in particular – by the time the Hapsburgs established dominance, the drama and beauty of the Baroque style was deemed the perfect tool to try and "impress" the local population and "persuade" them to come back into the fold (and if that didn't work, some were forced to convert or face the threat of exile or perhaps worse). And because the locals were **such** a tough sell, the rulers of the day employed the most beautiful, extravagant and voluminous Baroque their court architects could come up with. As a result, you'll find not only exceptionally dramatic and beautiful Baroque architecture in Prague (and in most Czech towns and villages, as well), but also a high concentration of it.

In Prague, most of the Renaissance-era structures of the Malá Strana district were demolished to make way for the palaces, churches and monasteries of the many noble families, Catholic orders and victorious generals of the Thirty Years' War who established themselves in Prague when the Hapsburgs took control. Talented artisans were brought in from all of the Hapsburg lands to work on the building projects along with the Italian Quarter's craftsmen, descended from the reign of Rudolf, who were at the ready to execute beautiful stucco work and wood and stone carving.

A New Century and a New Democracy

After the Counter-Reformation building boom wound down in the mid-18th century, a period of artistic austerity set in; a brief neo-Classical phase ensued. But the 19th century produced more extravagant architecture, including many structures that were part of the Czech cultural revival that emerged as the Austro-Hungarian Empire was in its last gasps. Some of these are the neo-Renaissance National Theater and the Art Nouveau Municipal House. A few Cubist structures followed.

With World War I and the disintegration of the Empire, Czechoslovakia, one of Europe's first democracies, was born. Its president, Tomaš Garrigue Masaryk, ushered in a new state that is known fondly by the Czechs as the "First Republic." The country was wealthy and well-educated and had state-of-the-art factories and a dense rail network thanks to the Austrians. Then Hitler decided he'd like to have it for himself.

Occupation

Partly because of the fact that thousands of ethnic Germans inhabited former Czechoslovakia's Sudetenland, and partly for other reasons, Hitler invaded and occupied the country but did not destroy it or Prague. That is one reason Prague's historic beauty is still relatively intact. But that's not to say that the population, the country and the economy didn't suffer terribly during the Nazi occupation. They suffered terribly, and the country's Jewish population suffered even more, with many paying the ultimate price: it is estimated that 90% of Czechoslovakia's Jews were killed in or en route to concentration camps, beginning their final journey with a stop at Terezín (Theresienstadt) in Northern Bohemia.

Of course, this is an oversimplification, but the Nazi occupation during World War II and the communist regime that followed just about did the country in – economically, socially, politically and culturally. Though the Czechs tried to reform the communist system in the 1960s with their "Prague Spring" and their dream of "socialism with a human face," they ended up paying a heavy price. In 1968, Soviet tanks rolled in to squash the dream, and during the period of Soviet occupation and "normalization" that followed, the nation's spirit was almost broken. Hopelessness and apathy set in.

Freedom

By the time Mikhail Gorbachev's perestroika provided a crack in the (Berlin) Wall just big enough for some East Germans to make it through to the grounds of the West German embassy in Prague, much had been lost in the Czech nation. But, at least the flood gates were finally opened, and one by one the communist regimes of Europe fell. In a sweet twist of fate, Václav Havel, the country's most prominent dissident and playwright who had spent years in communist jails, was swept into the presidency and into Prague Castle in December 1989.

The Prague I Knew

I arrived here in early 1992, to a still dark and mysterious city that looked like a fairytale stuck in time. Crumbling and weary though it was, its beauty was always evident and timeless. It had a character and atmosphere unique to that time, and a coal smoke patina that accentuated every detail of its buildings' elaborate stucco decorations that has now been lost. Prague has been all "cleaned up" and polished. And while I sometimes miss the "old" Prague that I came to, with its dark, gritty, gas-lit, coal-scented, empty-after-six-o'clock streets, I am glad for most of the changes.

Prague has transformed and is still transforming, but the amount of change that took place in the 1990s after I first arrived is staggering. A book like this about dining and shopping and modern art galleries and (many of the) fun things to do wouldn't have been possible then. While the city at that time was amazing, you would have just had to settle for whatever bland meal you could find (no salad, no fresh vegetables or fruit), and would have been limited to (always very beautiful and at that time very cheap) crystal and porcelain for souvenirs. But there always was plenty of excellent, cheap Czech beer to go around....

Naturally, this rich beauty and history, combined with the fact that Prague escaped a lot of the destruction of World War II, makes it an incredibly beautiful and popular tourist destination. It's estimated that more than 4.1 million international visitors come here annually, and you'll believe it when you walk with the throngs of tourists through the crowded streets of Old Town and Malá Strana.

And largely thanks to so much tourism, Prague is now flourishing in terms of dining, shopping, art and more. And since I am a major foodie, first things first: restaurants!

4 DINING OUT

As I mentioned in the Introduction, Prague is undergoing a transformation. And probably in no other area has it gone through a bigger change than in the area of dining. When I arrived here, not only was a good, tasty meal hard to come by, but sometimes **any** meal was hard to come by. Most restaurants were still state-owned, and often the staff would turn you away even with a room full of empty tables, saying simply, "We're full." So, you'd have to continue your search until you found a place that would even **serve** you.

A surer bet in those days was a typical Czech pub offering standard Czech fare. But the quality was not good, and you could be sure that you would be dining in a room so thick with cigarette smoke that sometimes your eyes would burn to the point of watering. And you could forget about variety and choice or any fresh vegetables (or, really, any vegetables at all other than boiled or pickled cabbage). Orange juice simply did not exist in the country, but Czech beer was always plentiful, cheap and wonderful. That is still the case for beer (though it's not as cheap as it once was). But it is still cheaper than water, Coke or, yes, the orange juice that I'm glad we have now!

These days, far from being associated with bland, heavy food, Prague has become known in some circles in Europe as a kind of "dining destination." The city center is packed with more restaurants than you would think could survive, owing to the huge numbers of tourists who visit year-round. And now – perhaps surprisingly, given the fact that many of the establishments cater to a captive tourist crowd – it's hard **not** to find a good meal in Prague. Still, some places are better than others. Some are unique and some are wonderful. And some are tourist traps. So my list of restaurants is intended to help you sift through the literally hundreds of choices you'll have. It is a sampling of some good, and/or trendy, places to eat in Prague, with convenient locations and varied cuisine. But first I'll mention some practical matters.

Reservations

While not always essential, it's a good idea to book ahead, especially at the popular places listed here (for places where it **is** essential, I've noted it). In most cases, I've provided phone numbers and websites with the listings. These are the most recent ones available, but in case any of them have changed, you can call information at 1180 (there should be English-speaking operators available) or check the websites I've provided. Also, note that the telephone country code for the Czech Republic is "420." Of course, when dialing within the country, you don't need it. You can always have your hotel concierge call for you, and I also offer Concierge Services for your stay in Prague.

Late Night Dining

Though the days have long passed when most kitchens closed at 9:00 PM, truly late night dining is still a bit difficult to come by. So, in case of after-theater or after-concert dinners, it's definitely best to reserve ahead – and order quickly once you arrive! (If you arrive after 9:30 PM, ask what time the kitchen closes.)

If Cigarette Smoke is a Problem

Smoking is still quite prevalent in the Czech Republic, and attempts to ban it in restaurants have failed so far. Well, that was the case until early 2017, when a law banning smoking in restaurants was FINALLY passed! HOWEVER, it has not gone into effect yet. That is supposed to happen in May. I'll believe it when I see it. Until then…

A few establishments offer no-smoking sections. However, these smoke-free areas are often smaller and less attractive than the smoking sections, as a majority of restaurants' patrons still smoke. Hence, it's common for the nicer dining spaces to be reserved for smokers. Furthermore, be aware that in many cases, the no-smoking section is right next to the smoking section, often even in the same room, with no walls or ventilation to make much of a difference.

So, if smoke is a concern for you while dining, my advice is to ask to see the non-smoking section when you get to the restaurant (or when you make your booking if you do so in person). See how it appeals to you and if it is properly divided from the smoking section. If you are planning to eat right then, check out whether it happens to be very smoky, even in the smoking section, as sometimes it can be hit or miss as to how many diners **actually are** smoking at any given time in any given place. Finally, a few Prague restaurants have taken the bold step of becoming "non-smoking restaurants," but they are still few and far between.

Prices, Credit Cards and Tipping

Given the exchange rates in recent years, restaurant meals in Prague, which used to be quite a bargain, are now priced more in line with restaurants in the U.S. or other parts of Western Europe, but Prague's prices are still cheaper. Within Prague the price range can vary greatly depending on location, type of food and style – and whether you order a Czech or imported wine. Therefore, rather than listing an approximate cost of a meal in any one restaurant, I've given each restaurant included here a designation as: **Very Expensive, Expensive, Moderate** or **Inexpensive.** These categories are meant to designate each restaurant's place relative to others in **Prague's** price scheme. Most restaurants post their menus with prices outside so that you can check out the prices before you enter.

Almost all restaurants and pubs in Prague accept major credit cards these days. MasterCard, Visa and Diners are the most widely-accepted, and in the center, a (very) few places accept American Express. And though Europe is moving to chip/PIN cards, you should have no trouble with cards that need to be swiped or with chip/sign. Many restaurants will also accept euros, so if you have some left over from a trip elsewhere, you might want to use this option. Ask your server. Of course, you won't get the best exchange rate, but in my experience, the rates haven't been terrible. Some menus will have prices listed in both Czech crowns and euros, usually an indication that they accept both, and that way you will see exactly how much you'll pay in euros should you want to do that.

When it comes to tipping, 10% is more than enough at nicer restaurants. There is no need to leave more than 10% – in fact, if you do, your waiter will either find it strange (and maybe even a little offensive!) or think that you made a mistake. In pubs and traditional Czech establishments, even 10% is a lot – the custom is to simply "round up" your bill: so, if your total is, say, CZK 166, you would make it CZK 170. The same tipping guidelines apply for taxis – in fact, if you give your driver a 10-crown tip regardless of the fare, he or she will be more than happy.

When paying for meals in cash, the server comes to your table and makes change on the spot, and you leave the tip by letting him know the amount he should give you change for. So, if your bill is 180 crowns and you want to leave, say, a 15-crown tip, tell him "195." Of course, if he or she doesn't speak English, you can just leave change on the table or hand the tip to your server.

When paying by credit card, you might have no other choice but to leave the tip in cash. In other cases you will have the option to enter a tip amount into the wireless terminal your waiter will bring to the table for charging your credit card (if you want to put the tip on your card, you must indicate this in advance!). Even if you're given this option, you still might want to leave the tip in cash, as there's a better chance your server will get it (this gesture is usually appreciated).

Some Dining Rules and Quirks

In contrast with the U.S., at least, you will not be rushed through your meal by your server. And, in fact, as I mention in the section on beer, many restaurants don't mind if you have only a drink. In general, unless a table is reserved for someone else at a certain time, you can linger for as long as you like without anyone raising an eyebrow. Likewise, if you have made a reservation for dinner, basically the table is yours for the night, and if you show up a little early or (even more than) a little late, as a rule, it will still be there empty and waiting for you when you arrive. The exceptions to this are the extremely popular spots, such as Sansho, where I've noted that reservations are **essential**.

On the other hand, don't be surprised if it's difficult to get your server's attention, even when you want to pay. So, if you need to rush off to a concert, don't wait until the last minute to ask for your bill. It is hit or miss – you could get it right away or you could wait quite a while. It all depends on how busy the staff is, as even collecting money is not always a priority. Sadly, all too often many waiters and waitresses here are known to employ incredible tunnel vision.

Sometimes they also have tunnel thinking: if they pass your table while taking food to someone else, and you motion or call to them in an effort to get them to simply **stop by** your table on their way back, don't be surprised if you get a look and a reply that basically means, "Can't you see I'm busy?!" The idea of even **acknowledging** one guest while on the way to serve another one is not always understood. In any case, when you want to pay, say "Zaplatím" ("I'll pay") or ask for the bill ("účet," pronounced "oochet"). **In general, you will not be asked to pay until you ask for the bill.**

In almost all restaurants and pubs, your glass of water, wine or beer, or your cup of coffee, will not be taken away until every last drop of liquid has been consumed. If there is anything left in it, your server will not remove it from your table. When it's getting low, they **might** ask if you'd like another ("ještě jedno?"), but even if they bring another beer or glass of wine, they will not take the first one if there's anything left in it (unless you tell them to).

When it comes to food, your plate will not be taken away until you have placed both your fork and knife together on the plate at the 4:00 position. Once you do this, your plate will be whisked away as soon as the configuration is spotted, with almost lightning speed! So, if you are not finished, don't put your cutlery in this position! Instead, keep them apart at opposite angles – this is a signal that you have not finished your meal. Until you have put your cutlery at 4:00, no one will ask you "are you finished?" even if every morsel of food is gone from your plate – and you will also therefore wait… for your plate to be taken, to order dessert, to get your bill and pay, etc.

So, now that you've got some practical information, here is my list of recommended restaurants. Mostly they are arranged by area of town, but I also have a few sections for special types of cuisine or special features.

Restaurants in Old Town

Kogo – Mainly Italian, with some Yugoslav specialties thrown in. Though it used to boast better value for money, Kogo is still one of Prague's most popular spots. Great soups, pasta and roasted baby lamb, as well as fresh seafood and good wines. Run by Bosnian immigrants – a real success story.

I will say, however, that in recent years I have noticed that the place is looking a bit worn, and the wait staff might be exhausted from all their success, as a few times lately they have had a bad attitude. It seems to be hit or miss. But I still have it listed, **especially for summer months**, as the courtyard of the Slovanský Dům location is one of the most pleasant spots in Prague to dine outdoors. Kogo's two main locations are:

• **Slovanský Dům** (my favorite) at Na Příkopě 22, near Obecní Dům (the Municipal House). Lots of outdoor dining is available in a beautiful courtyard in the spring and summer, and even in cooler months with heat lamps. Very popular and with a good atmosphere. Convenient for pre-concert dinners if you're going to Obecní Dům. The kitchen might be open late enough for after-concert dining, but I would check first.

www.kogo.cz/en
Price range: Expensive
Phone: 221-451-259
Metro: Náměstí Republiky (yellow or "B" line)
Tram: 6, 8, 15, and 26 to Náměstí Republiky

• **Havelská Street,** the original Kogo at Havelská 27, close to Old Town Square and the Estates Theater (Stavovské Divadlo). Very convenient for pre-opera dinners in case you're seeing something at the Estates.

Phone: 224-214-543
Metro: Můstek (green or "A" line and yellow or "B" line)

V Zátiší – At Betlémské Náměstí/Liliová 1, this chic, modern restaurant serves an impressive and unlikely mix of nouvelle cuisine (Czech, continental and Indian). It's quite expensive but good, and in keeping with the nouvelle cuisine tradition, don't expect big portions. The décor is impressive, and V Zátiší has come a long since my arrival in 1992 when every expat in town dined there often because it was the only restaurant in Prague that had lettuce.

www.vzatisi.cz
Price range: Expensive
Phone: 222 221 155
Tram: 2, 9, 17, 18, 22 to Národní Třída

No Stress Café – This spot used to be decorated with furniture from Le Patio (see "Shopping and Souvenirs"), and the décor added a lot to the ambiance and dining experience. But in 2016 they decided to redecorate. While the No Stress kitchen still offers top-rate, very fresh Asian-French "fusion" cuisine accompanied by a decent wine list (including fairly good wines by the glass), the experience is just not the same without the comfortable leather armchairs that used to dot the place. And the service is not as friendly and professional as it used to be either. However, it's still a good choice if you're in the vicinity of the Spanish Synagogue. Located across from the Spanish Synagogue at Dušní 10/Kolkovně 9, Prague 1.

www.nostress.cz
Price range: Moderate to Expensive
Phone: 222-317-007
Metro: Staroměstská (green or "A" line)
Tram: 17 to Právnická Falkulta

Ristorante Pasta Fresca – part of the Ambiente chain of restaurants. Great steaks, homemade pasta, and some of the lightest gnocchi around. They also have a very good wine list and sommelier. Celetná 11 just off of Old Town Square.

www.ambi.cz
Price range: Moderate
Phone: 224-230-244
Metro: Můstek (green or "A" line and yellow or "B" line), followed by a 3-minute walk to Old Town Square.

Divinis Wine Bar – this cozy yet refined Old Town spot serves some of the finest, most authentic Italian meals you'll find outside of Italy. It's pricey but highly recommended and has very good service. **Reservations are essential. Closed Sundays.**

www.divinis.cz
Price range: Expensive
Phone: 222-325 440
Metro: Staroměstská (green or "A" line) or Náměsti Republiky (yellow or "B" line), with a 3-4 minute walk required from either stop.

Red Pif – One of the newest entries on Prague's restaurant scene, this French eatery offers a trendy, artsy dining space and an excellent wine list. Red Pif has daily offerings of a wide selection of (mostly French) wines **by the glass**, as well (**decent** wines **by the glass** are still not so common in Prague). They will also let you taste several wines and will share their expert advice in helping you choose just the right wine for you, even if you only want to have a glass or two and nothing else. Betlémská 9, Old Town (entrance at U Dobřenských Street 1).

www.redpif.cz
Price range: Moderate
Phone: 222-232-086
Tram: 2, 9, 18, 22 to Národní Třída or 2 or 18 to Karlovy Lázně

Sansho at Petrská 25 in New Town (Nové Město) – This relatively new place has made a big splash on the Prague restaurant scene. Many of my fellow foodie friends say it is their favorite restaurant in Prague. And now that I have tried it, I can say the same. Chef Paul Day, described as a "chef, butcher and urban meat roasting specialist," has opened this restaurant with a philosophy "based on honest food, the best ingredients, knowledge and fun." They serve a six-course degustation menu specially prepared each night based on the ingredients they've sourced for around CZK 900 per person. Pricey but very highly recommended. **Reservations are essential**.

www.sansho.cz
Price range: Very Expensive
Phone: 222-317-425
Metro: Florenc (red or "C" line)
Tram: 3, 8, 14 or 24 to Bílá Labut'

La Finestra at Platnéřská 90 in Old Town (Staré Město) – This sister to Aromi (see the section on the 'Burbs) was opened in 2009 as the second restaurant of Italian chef Riccardo Lucque. Whereas Aromi is all about fish, La Finestra is more about meat. And it's one of the trendiest and best places to eat in Old Town. **Essential to book ahead.** Very pricey but many of the well-to-do locals love it.

www.lafinestra.cz
Price range: Very Expensive
Phone: 222-325-325
Metro: Staroměstská (green or "A" line)
Tram: 2, 17 or 18 to Staroměstská

Pastacaffé – Part of the Ambiente restaurant group. Serving great pastas, salads and sandwiches. I like it for a nice, inexpensive lunch stop. Located next to the Spanish Synagogue and across from No Stress Café at Vězeňská 1.

www.ambi.cz
Price range: Moderate
Phone: 224-813-257

Metro: Staroměstská (green or "A" line)
Tram: 17 to Právnická Falkulta

Restaurants in Malá Strana

Kampa Park at Na Kampě 8b, Prague 1, Malá Strana – Many consider this to be Prague's best restaurant. It has excellent cuisine and service, and is frequented by politicians and celebrities, both domestic and foreign, if there happen to be any in town. I will say, however, that the quality of the food has gone down a notch in recent years (though it's still very good) while the prices have gone up several. But, the beautiful views of the Charles Bridge from one of the many outdoor or indoor tables on the river are the real reason to visit. Kampa runs a group of restaurants (including Hergetová Cihelna below). Located on beautiful Kampa Island just under the Charles Bridge.

www.kampagroup.com
Price range: Very Expensive
Phone: 296-826-112
Metro: Malostranská (green or "A" line)
Tram: 12, 15, 20 and 22 to Malostranské Náměstí

Hergetová Cihelna – near Kampa Park at Cihelna 2b, Malá Strana, this place also has beautiful views of the Charles Bridge. If the weather is nice, ask to sit on the terrace. If not, try to get a table with a view of the Charles Bridge from inside. (Be aware that terrace tables can be hard to come by, as they are booked well in advance, and members of their dining club get priority seating!) Good food and usually good service; interesting dishes, including modern variations of traditional Czech cuisine; and cheaper than Kampa Park.

www.kampagroup.com
Price range: Moderate to Expensive
Phone: 296 826 103
Metro: Malostranská (green or "A" line)
Tram: 12, 15, 20 and 22 to Malostranské Náměstí

Café Savoy – part of the Ambiente group of restaurants, Café Savoy has an interesting menu selection of well-prepared "modernized" Czech fare and continental dishes. They also have a very good wine list and sommelier. Great cakes and other desserts, including traditional Czech ones, made in the patisserie downstairs (which you can view behind a glass wall on your way to the restrooms) also make it a good place for dessert and coffee – or for a traditional, high-quality Hungarian Tokaj dessert wine.

Here you can try "real" svíčková for a very traditional Czech main dish if they happen to have it on offer ("real" means it is made with the correct/better cut of meat, which you won't find in cheaper pubs), and apple strudel or a větrník (something like an éclair, or the Czech/Austro-Hungarian version of it) for dessert. And if you sense that your waiter or waitress is a bit snooty in this place, it's not your imagination. Still, I continue to love it for the food and atmosphere. The dining rooms, especially the beautifully decorated ceilings, are stunning. Vítězná 5.

www.ambi.cz
Price range: Moderate to Expensive
Phone: 257-311-562.
Tram: 9, 12, 15, 20 or 22 to Újezd

Ichnusa – this very local place (at least the tourists hadn't discovered it the last time I was there, but, as with all things in Prague, you'd better hurry!) is a wonderful little Sardinian restaurant, with a friendly, very helpful staff and an owner who takes personal care in your enjoying your visit as well as in helping you select from the great wines he has on offer. Ichnusa serves lots of fresh seafood (the fish is either grilled or baked to perfection) and wonderful appetizers and pasta.

While Ichnusa is a very lively and trendy place, it also has a down-home feel (if you're there for a late lunch, you might spot the chef and the entire wait-staff sitting down at a table eating their own cooking once they are sure you're toward the end of your meal). And they don't mind if you linger, either. A very special place. Around the corner from Café Savoy at Plaska 5. **Closed Sundays.**

www.ichnusabotegabistro.cz
Price range: Moderate to Expensive
Phone: 605-375-012
Tram: 9, 15, 12, 20 or 22 to Újezd

Café de Paris – Keeping it simple, this more or less Parisian-style café offers basically one dish: Entrecôte "Cafe de Paris" covered with their own secret-recipe "Cafe de Paris" sauce served with fabulous French fries, a French baguette, and a green salad dressed with a light vinaigrette. This dish (including that secret sauce!) is really good, and the fries are fabulous. Unusually for the center of Prague, they do not accept credit cards.

www.cafedeparis.cz
Price range: Moderate to Expensive
Phone: 603 160 718
Tram: 12, 15, 20 or 22 to Helichova or to Malostranské Náměstí

Czech Fare

High quality traditional Czech food, which has a not-always-deserved reputation of being bland and heavy, is, believe it or not, becoming hard to find in Old Town. The rush to "modernize," along with the desire to explore varied cuisine after 40 years of pork and cabbage, has led many restaurateurs and chefs to shun local fare for the more sophisticated and exotic. While some of the above restaurants offer a few Czech dishes, and there are still a few traditional pubs around, most of the Czech restaurants in the center of town are either tourist traps or of low quality or both.

But assuming you would like the adventure of trying what

I'll describe as the "hearty, Central European fare" that I've actually come to love, I've listed some of my (and my Czech friends') favorite places below. I do believe that once you develop a taste for fluffy Czech bread dumplings (houskové knedlíky) and crispy, roasted duck (pečená kachna), you'll start to crave it. Here are a few choices:

U Medvídků at Na Perštýně 7, near Tesco off of Národní Třída, is one of the few traditional pubs left in Old Town, but it's now **very** touristy. It's also one of the few places in Prague that serves (the original) Budweiser or Budvar.

www.umedvidku.cz
Price range: Inexpensive to Moderate
Phone: 224-211-916
Tram: 2, 9, 18, 22 to Národní Třída

V Kolkovně – across the street from No Stress Café and the Spanish Synagogue. This place offers traditional Czech dishes and ample Pilsner Urquell beer. Kolkovna is part of the "Pilsner Urquell Original Restaruant" chain which is owned and operated by the famous Pilsner Urquell brewery (located in the town of Pilsen, where the word "pilsner" comes from). The food is very good, but be aware that the place is designed for tourists, is huge, and is often over-crowded. And the waiters, knowing they have a captive clientele, are not always the friendliest. But if you want good goulash, crispy duck, and decent dumplings, this is a good place. V Kolkovně 8.

www.vkolkovne.cz
Phone: 224-819-701
Price range: Moderate
Metro: Staroměstská (green or "A" line)
Tram: 17 to Právnická Falkulta

Olympia – This is another of the Pilsner Urquell restaurant chain's locations (across from Café Savoy mentioned previously). The goulash at Olympia is wonderful, with impossibly dark sauce, which was voted the best in town in a recent Prague Post "Best of Prague" survey. Vítězná 7.

www.kolkovna.cz
Phone: 251-511-080
Price range: Inexpensive to Moderate
Tram: 9, 12, 15, 20 or 22 to Újezd

Malostranská Beseda - Malostranské Náměstí 21. This pub has really good Czech food and fresh Pilsner Urquell beer, all at reasonable prices, especially considering its prime location on Malostranské Náměstí. Outdoor tables on the square are available most months of the year (with heat lamps and blankets when necessary).

www.malostranska-beseda.cz
Price range: Inexpensive to Moderate
Phone: 257 409 112
Tram: 12, 15, 20 and 22 to Malostranské Náměstí

Lokál – Dlouhá 33 (Old Town) and Míšeňská 12 (Malá Strana). This relatively new place offers a modern version of a traditional Czech pub. The food is very good, and the atmosphere is lively, with a young crowd drawn to the cheap Pilsner Urquell beer served from tanks (see "Speaking of Beer"). Their staff tries hard, too, even offering extra sauce with your particular dish if they notice that you don't have enough in which to soak your dumplings (which, by the way, are the best bread dumplings in Prague). Part of the Ambiente chain (see Café Savoy).

www.ambi.cz
Price range: Inexpensive to Moderate

• **Old Town Location:**
  Phone: 222-316-265
  Tram: 6, 8, 15, and 26 to Dlouhá Třída
  Metro: Náměstí Republiky (yellow or "B" line).

- **Mala Strana Location:**
  Phone: 257-212-014
  Tram: 12, 15, 20 and 22 to Malostranské Náměstí

Speaking of Beer

Czech beer is simply delicious, and the Czechs drink more beer per capita than any nation on earth. Some workers even have it in the morning! Many consider Pilsner Urquell (Plzeňský Prazdroj) to be the best Czech beer, or even the best beer in the world. All pubs will have a sign outside displaying the brand(s) of beer they serve. I can't think of any restaurants in Prague that don't serve beer (though there might be a few), so you can find many places just to sit for a "velké pivo" (large beer) served by the half liter. A small beer ("malé pivo") is 0.33 liter. And most restaurants don't mind if you have only a drink and no food if you just want an afternoon refresher after a day of touring!

In recent years, many of the large Czech breweries have been experimenting with variations on their old traditional lagers and dark beers, and the microbrewery fad has hit the Czech Republic, too, with great results. So, for example, many of the restaurants serving Staropramen (the brand from an old Prague brewery) now also offer wheat beers and unfiltered beers. And if you want to sample many different brews from several microbreweries, look for "Beerpoints." A good place is Nota Bene near the IP Pavlova metro and tram (4, 6, 10, 11, 13, 16, and 22) stop. Náš Váš Svět and Pivo a Párek a little further out Korunní in Vinohrady serve several good microbrews on tap (take tram 10 or 16 to the Perunova stop).

Beer from the tank (pivo z tanku) is another of the latest trends in brewing and serving beer in the Czech Republic. Lokál is one pub that serves its Pilsner Urquell from the tank, which is fresher than keg or bottled beer because it moves from the brewery to the tap within a few hours. And because of the way it's packaged and stored, tank beer doesn't have to be pasteurized (and must be consumed within two weeks, which does not prove difficult in the Czech Republic). The tanks at Lokál will be clearly marked with the date on which the content of each was shipped from the brewery in Pilsen.

Another place to check out is the famous U Fleků (Křemencova 11, Prague 1, near Karlovo Náměstí). While it's **quite** touristy these days, it is still a remarkable place: They have been brewing their own beer here since 1499, or only a few years after Christopher Columbus set sail on his famous voyage, as their website proudly points out. Take tram 5 to Myslíkova or trams 2, 3, 4, 6, 10, 14, 16, 18, 22 or 24 or Metro yellow ("B") line to Karlovo Náměstí.

In the summer, the beer garden in Letná Park up on the Letná plain is a great place to be. Sit under shady trees on a sunny day with locals, children, dogs and rollerbladers and drink all the beer you want served from kegs at outdoor stands. Don't be surprised to see a wedding party or two pass by. Located in Letenské Sady. To get there, you can either build up your thirst by walking up the (very) steep hill across the Vltava River from Pařížská Street in Old Town, or take a tram (1, 2, 8, 12, 14, 25, 26) to Letenské Náměstí and walk 3-5 minutes to the park overlooking the river.

What about Czech wine, you might ask? My view is: don't bother. If you're not a beer drinker, order yourself a nice bottle of imported wine from almost anywhere else!

OK, that was a bit harsh, but the truth is, it doesn't get warm and sunny enough here to produce great wines. But if you want to try it, Café Savoy and Red Pif can steer you to some nice choices.

If You Want to Venture Out to the 'Burbs

Many of Prague's best restaurants are located out of the city center, offering a more local experience. Here are a few notable places:

Osteria Da Clara – Mexická 7. Prague 10, in Vršovice. This local find is so good, my friends asked me not to list it – it's already hard to get a table without tourists knowing about it! This is a very down home, family-run Italian osteria. Great wines and daily specials at great prices with personal, friendly service. Lunch only on Sundays. Kitchen closes for a few hours in the late afternoon on other days. **Essential to reserve for evenings,** and a good idea at lunch.

www.daclara.com
Price range: Moderate
Phone: 271-726-548
Tram: 4 or 22 to Ruská, then continue four blocks east on Ruská to Mexická.

Aromi – located near the Vinohrady Theater at Náměstí Míru 6. Aromi serves Italian cuisine, including lots of fresh seafood cooked to order in a very international dining atmosphere. Aromi is a sister restaurant to La Finestra in Old Town. Best to book ahead.

www.aromi.cz
Price range: Moderate to Expensive
Phone: 222-713-222
Metro: Náměstí Míru (green or "A" line)
Tram: 4, 10, 16, or 22 to Náměstí Míru

See also "Mailsi," and "Masala," under "Ethnic Cuisine."

Nota Bene – located near Náměstí Míru at Mikovcova 4, Prague 2. This is one of the better places for a new take on traditional Czech food. Not only is it a good restaurant, with very fresh local and innovative dishes, it's also one of the new "Beerpoints" that have been popping up lately. It offers daily specials made with meat from The Real Meat Society (a butcher shop run by Sansho's chef offering fantastic quality organic and/or free range meat) and various beers from the Unětický, Kocour and Matuška microbreweries. Don't try to go here without a reservation.

While the food at Nota Bene is very good, I would offer these caveats: The service can be iffy, and if you go there for lunch, you'd better make your reservation for an early hour (which in Prague means 11:30 or 12:00). This is a very Czech, very local place, and Czechs eat lunch early (usually around 11:30). Also, traditional Czech places offer daily lunch specials, for which restaurants prepare only a limited amount, so if you get there late, often the specials, which are cheaper, will be sold out (if that is the case, at most places you can still order from the regular – pricier – menu). However, Nota Bene offers only specials at lunch, and only four of them at that. So, if you go later, say even at 12:30 or 1:00, you run a real risk that many of the daily offers will be sold out, severely limiting your choice.

Though it is true that Nota Bene sources its ingredients fresh daily, resulting in very good, fresh dishes, one wonders why they simply don't buy and prepare more, given their demand. In the evenings, you order from the regular menu, and so far availability doesn't seem to be as much of a problem at night. But I have rarely been to Nota Bene at lunch when at least one dish was not already sold out, and I've usually been there at 12:30 or 1:00 at the latest. This is not the case for the other restaurants I've listed here (though the "pubs" like Lokál or Malostranská Beseda might run out of a particular dish or two by around 2:00 PM, especially duck). **Closed Sundays. No credit cards. Kitchen closes in the afternoons from 3:00-6:00.**

www.notabene-restaurant.cz
Price range: Moderate
Phone: 721-299-131
Tram: 4, 10, 11, 13, 16, 22 to IP Pavlova
Metro: IP Pavlova (red or "C" line)

Outdoor Dining

In the spring and summer, Prague has hundreds of spots for outdoor dining. But many of them are, unfortunately, very touristy, if not outright tourist traps. And they are often located in crowded, noisy spots (such as Old Town Square and Karlova Street). For quieter outdoor dining and/or locations with great views, here are a few of my top picks (details on all of these places are listed elsewhere in this chapter):

• **Kogo** (Slovanský Dům location) has a beautiful, leafy courtyard that is a peaceful oasis in the heart of the crowded city.

• **Kampa Park** and **Hergetova Cihelna** are both situated on the Vltava River in Mala Strana. Their riverfront terraces offer stunning views of the Charles Bridge.

• **U Prince** on Old Town Square has a rooftop terrace that offers stunning views of the Old Town Hall and Týn Church (along with mediocre food and service).

• **Da Clara** in Vršovice usually has sidewalk tables in the summer.

Just keep in mind that the timing of when a particular restaurant actually sets up its outdoor tables each year depends on the whim (and approval) of some city official who might not get around to it until well into the outdoor dining season. Of course, you can spot this easily enough, but I wanted to warn you in case you travel out to the 'burbs expecting a certain place to have outdoor tables set up just because "they should by now."

Ethnic Cuisine

When it comes to "ethnic" cuisine, Prague, unfortunately, has not yet reached the high level in terms of options and/or quality that you'll find in some other European capitals, like London or Berlin. And where some cuisines, like Indian for example, are known in other cities for their affordability, in

Prague, it can be just the opposite. However, this dining sector has undergone somewhat of a boom here recently, and there are a few very notable exceptions if you'd like some variety and spice during your trip.

The Sushi Bar – Zborovská 49, across the street from Café Savoy and next to Olympia. Having been here 12 years now, this was one of the first serious sushi places in Prague, and it is undoubtedly the best. The chef trained for many years in Japan, and the quality is top notch, almost as good as what you'll find in New York or Tokyo. And the prices reach nearly the same levels, too.

www.sushi.cz
Price range: Expensive
Phone: 603-244-882
Tram: 9, 12, 15, 20, or 22 to Újezd

Noi – On Újezd in Malá Strana. This is one of the best and one of the most popular Thai restaurants in Prague. The dishes tend to go beyond the usual chicken satay and pad thai kai, and the range of spices tends to go beyond the usual, as well. There's an outdoor garden in the spring and summer. Unfortunately, Noi can get very smoky indoors, so if you're not able to dine outside (the outdoor tables fill up quickly), this can be a problem, especially at peak dinner hours. So, if smoke is a real problem for you, try it for lunch or an early dinner, when it tends to be less busy (or sit outdoors if weather and space permit). Reservations are recommended, especially for dinner. Újezd 19, Malá Strana.

www.noirestaurant.cz
Phone: 257-311-411
Price range: Moderate to Expensive
Tram: 9, 12, 15, 20, and 22 to Újezd or 12, 15, 20 and 22 to Hellichova

Mailsi Pakistani Restaurant – Lipanská 1. This family-run, homey place serves wonderfully cooked Tandoori meats in (very) rich, (very) creamy sauces in Prague's edgy Žižkov neighborhood. While the prices are a little on the high side compared to similar cuisine in other cities, it's still one of my favorites.

www.mailsi.cz
Price range: Moderate to Expensive
Phone: 774-972-010
Tram: 5, 9, 15, or 26 to Lipanská

Masala – Jana Masaryka 36 in Prague 2. This Indian restaurant has quickly become very popular. It has reasonable prices, tasty dishes and a colorful décor. Don't even think about going without a reservation, unless you arrive really early, like 6:00 PM. **Note:** The last time I was there, Masala had a new staff and a new menu. Perhaps they have a new chef, too, because the food was noticeably not as good as previously. And now it has a new location, too (I have not yet tried the Jana Masaryka location listed here). I'm leaving Masala in this book for now, but you might want to check TripAdvisor before heading there.

www.masala.cz
Price range: Moderate
Phone: 222-251-601
Metro: Naměstí Míru (green or "A" line)
Tram: 4 or 22 to Jana Masaryka

Vegetarian and Vegan

Country Life – Melantrichova Street in Old Town. This is one of the few vegetarian/vegan choices in the land of pork and dumplings (the Czech Republic has the highest per capita consumption of pork – and beer – in the world). It's a local and tourist healthy favorite with a convenient, central location. Country Life is buffet style and you pay by weight, with fantastic fresh-squeezed carrot juice. They also have many gluten-free choices (check with a server about gluten-free offerings).

www.countrylife.cz
Price range: Inexpensive to Moderate
Metro: Můstek (green or "A" and yellow or "B" lines)

Loving Hut – Several locations, including: Na Poříčí 25 in the Černá Labuť building (near Naměstí Republiky), Londýnská 35 (in Vinohrady) and Plzenská 8 (Prague 5, in the Anděl shopping center). This popular chain of buffet restaurants offers fresh, vegan fare.

www.lovinghut.cz
Price range: Inexpensive

On the Go

There are also many eat-in pizzerias and other low-cost eateries throughout Prague. So if you just want a quick, cheap meal, you can certainly find it. When it comes to take-away, I find most of the by-the-slice pizza and gyros places to be of rather low quality. But one exception is Giallo Rossa Pizza on Jakubská in Old Town (around the corner from Sv. Jakub church) and on Vinohradská in Vinohrady (at the Jiřího z Poděbrad metro station on the green line). And there's always grilled klobasa sausage served with a slice of bread and mustard from street stands and at occasional street fairs.

Old World Cafes

Traditional Central European café culture as it still exists to some extent in cities like Vienna was, unfortunately, undone by the communist regime here and has never fully recovered. But for a semblance of what once was the particular Austro-Hungarian version in Prague, the following places come closest (although, unfortunately, for sheer quality of coffee, and in some cases atmosphere, places like Ebel and Starbucks are sometimes better):

Café Imperial – Na Poříčí. This is actually a fairly good restaurant in a former Old World café, serving breakfast, lunch and dinner. The food is quite good (it's a partner with Divinis Wine Bar, though not of that quality) while the coffee is just OK. But it's worth a visit to see the original, elaborate ceramic tile décor that was, fortunately, left intact throughout all the dreary communist years.

www.cafeimperial.cz
Price range: Moderate to Expensive
Phone: 246-011-440
Metro: Náměstí Republiky (yellow or "B" line)
Tram: 3, 8, 14, 24 to Bílá Labuť

Café Slavia – Národní Třída. This was once a haunt of Czech intellectuals, including the dissident playwright and former Czech president Václav Havel. Now it is mostly a tourist haunt, but the views of the Vltava (Moldau) river and Prague Castle offered through its huge windows are still spectacular. Visit for the views and the nostalgia, not for the heavily microwaved and overpriced food.

www.cafeslavia.cz
Price range: Moderate
Phone: 224-218-493
Tram: 2, 9, 17, 18, or 22 to Národní Divadlo

Kavarna Lucerna – In the Lucerna Pasáž on Vodičkova Street, near Wenceslas Square. This spacious café is located in the wonderful Art Nouveau Lucerna Pasáž, which was built by the grandfather of the former Czech President and dissident Václav Havel. The café (and the movie theater to which it leads, as well as the entire passage) is one of the most authentic and unique of its kind. Stepping into it is like stepping back in time. Plus, you can view the hanging inverted horse statue by David Černy from the café's large, arched windows. This place usually has lots of smokers.

Price range: Moderate

Tram: 3, 5, 6, 9, 14, or 24 to Vodičkova
Metro: Můstek (green or "A" line and yellow or "B" line)

Cukrárna Myšák (Patisserie Mysak) – At Vodičkova 31, near Wenceslas Square. This café is newly opened but in an Old World style. Experience the luxury of crystal chandeliers and mirrored dining rooms while you indulge in one of the many cakes or (huge) ice cream concoctions that you've chosen from the beautiful display cases full of eye-popping and tasty-looking deserts.

Price range: Moderate
Tram: 3, 5, 6, 9, 14, or 24 to Vodíčkova
Metro: Můstek (green or "A" line and yellow or "B" line)

Café Louvre – Národní Třída, close to Tesco at the corner of Spálená. Louvre is quite popular for lunch and meeting up with friends. The interior space gives a hint of what once was.

www.cafelouvre.cz
Price range: Moderate
Phone: 224-930-949
Tram: 2, 9, 18, 22 to Národní Třída

Kavárna Obecní Dům (Municipal House Café) – located in the Obecní Dům on Náměstí Republiky. This place calls itself "Prague's most beautiful café." This is probably true. It is also now mainly a tourist trap. But that doesn't mean you shouldn't go there to at least have a look and maybe even sit for a drink and to soak up the uniquely beautiful surroundings. Just don't expect great coffee or cakes, and you probably won't get great service, either. Still, it's not horrible, and the stunning original Art Nouveau interior gives the feel of an old European grand café.

Price range: Moderate to Expensive
Metro: Náměstí Republiky (yellow or "B" line)
Tram: 6, 8, 15, and 26 to Náměstí Republiky

Newer Cafes

Ebel Coffee – two locations, both in Old Town: Kaprova Street, just off Old Town Square, and Řetězová Street, off of Husova Street (not far from Karlova Street). Arguably, this is the best coffee in Prague. Ebel imports and roasts its own beans and makes excellent blends for espresso, cappuccino, etc., in attractive locations and settings (the Kaprova Street location is mainly take-away but has a few stools inside.

Price range: Moderate
Metro: Staroměstská (green or "A" line)
Tram: 2, 17 and 18 to Staroměstská

Bake Shop Praha – a very high quality American-style bakery with sandwiches, salads and cookies, excellent croissants (the best I've ever had, actually, including those I've had in Paris), quiche, and wonderful carrot cake (the "best in the world," according to one customer and their menu) and other goodies. On Kozí 1 at the corner of Dlouhá in Old Town.

www.bakeshop.cz
Price range: Moderate to Expensive
Phone: 222-316-823
Metro: Náměstí Republiky (yellow or "B" line)
Tram: 6, 8, 15 and 26 to Dlouhá Třída

Starbucks – Yes, we have them now. You can't miss Starbucks' first location in the Czech Republic: on Malostranské Náměstí right at the 12, 15, 20, and 22 tram stop. They offer the same drinks as all their other stores around the world, plus free unlimited Wi-Fi. Some other locations are on Old Town Square (across from the astronomical clock), on Wenceslas Square (two of them), in the Palladium shopping mall and at Prague Airport Terminal 1, in case you want a fix for your jetlag when you arrive or need something to do after you've checked in for your flight home.

www.starbuckscoffee.cz

Ice Cream

In case you get a hankering for Italian gelato while you're in Prague, even though you're not in Italy…

While walking the streets of Prague, you'll find ice cream for sale just about everywhere. This is true even in the winter, but in the summer, extra street stands appear in big numbers. While all of the ice cream piled high on display looks good, the quality of the street card variety ranges from mediocre to just OK. So if you are willing to resist the temptation of the stuff beckoning you on the city's squares and instead put in a little effort to seek out either of the two places recommended below, you will be greatly rewarded with some of the best gelato to be had anywhere. These two places rival each other for the top spot in Prague:

Angelato – By far, this is my favorite place for ice cream in Prague. It is billed as "all natural" ice cream, (though I am not sure of the exact specifications, but it certainly tastes very "natural"). And it also tastes incredibly fresh. That's because they make each flavor fresh every morning, which means that if you get there later in the evening they might be out of a lot of their choices – you won't find them restocking it from the freezer late in the day to have it sit there overnight. Angelato also does wonderful seasonal flavors, so there's always something new. In the autumn you might find cinnamon, pear and sage, or poppy seed flavor. This past spring they had rhubarb, and for asparagus season, yes, they had asparagus flavor. They are always experimenting, while also serving the usual vanilla, chocolate, and the best pistachio I've ever tasted. Rytířská 27 in Old Town. (Angelato recently added a new location in Mala Strana at Újezd 24.)

www.angelato.cz
Phone: 224-235-123

Metro: Mustek (green or "A" line and yellow or "B" line)
Tram: 2, 9, 18, 22 to Národní Třída, followed by a short walk,
    or a short walk from Old Town Square

Crème de la Crème – This is the only rival to Angelato, and the quality of this ice cream is fantastic also. The owner spent five years in Italy perfecting the art of making great gelato, and it shows. Crème de la Crème tends to focus on the more traditional flavors, though it also has some unusual flavors and combinations. And the consistency of their gelato is a bit creamier than Angelato's. I would suggest you try this place and Angelato, and then you can be the judge! On Husova Street in Old Town.

Tram: 2, 9, 18, 22 to Národní Třída, followed by a short walk,
    or a short walk from Old Town Square.

Notes

_____
_____
_____
_____
_____
_____
_____
_____
_____
_____
_____
_____
_____
_____
_____
_____
_____
_____
_____
_____
_____
_____
_____
_____
_____
_____
_____
_____

5 SHOPPING AND SOUVENIRS

Crystal and Fine Glass

The Czech Republic is famous for its crystal and glass. There are crystal shops everywhere – on every corner and several on each block. You would think they couldn't all survive, yet more of them keep opening. The quality is, for the most part, very good and the prices are quite low (though they have gone up in recent years, so the deals aren't as good as they used to be). Still, good crystal is quite cheap here, and most shops will ship it for you if you end up buying too much to carry (for a fee, of course, but you will save the VAT, which can be almost 20%).

Erpet – This is a great shop on Old Town Square. It has a **huge** variety and selection of crystal and porcelain (for which the Czechs are also rather famous).

Erpet also carries Czech garnets ("granát"). Years ago there were only a few shops specializing in jewelry made with this stone, and they were quite reliable. But now there is an explosion of garnet shops that are mainly rip-off places. My advice is to stay away from them and to see what Erpet has on offer.

Note: If you might be interested in crystal or garnets and more, email me at **krysti.brice@seznam.cz** and I can send you **discount coupons** for Erpet or I can leave some for you at your hotel once you arrive.

www.erpetcrystal.cz

Moser, produced in the spa town of Karlovy Vary (Carlsbad), is considered by some to be the finest crystal in the world, on a par with or better than Waterford, and it is quite pricey, even by the relatively cheaper crystal prices in the Czech Republic. It is much more expensive than Bohemia Crystal and other Czech brands. And you can see and feel the difference – Moser is more than "a cut above."

Moser is available at Erpet, but for a unique experience, visit the original Moser store on Na Příkopě, a bit of Old World luxury and charm which survived even the communist times (and has now been substantially refurbished). Moser also has a newer store on Old Town Square.

www.moser-glass.com

The Czechs also produce an endless array of high-quality, hand-blown glass. It is, of course, cheaper than the crystal, but the quality of Czech glass is also evident. Most crystal shops carry a range of fine glass in addition to crystal. A few makers of unique pieces of "art" glass and "designer" crystal have their own shops showcasing their work. Some of the best places to look are:

Material – This is one of the best art glass makers, located in Týnský Dvůr (Ungelt) where Dr. Stewart's Botanicus is also located (see below). These unique pieces are very special, as is the shop itself.

www.i-material.com

Artěl – Try not to miss this exclusive design shop featuring current versions of classic Czech design items. An American artist from New York founded Artěl in 1998, and she has done some amazing things with her collection. Artěl's products are very unique, combining the exquisite quality of mouth-blown, hand-decorated, 100% lead-free crystal with sophisticated, modern design. The main store is located just behind Obecní Dům and Hotel Paříž on Rybná Street. Two newer locations are located in Malá Strana just below the Charles Bridge and on Platnéřská Street in Old Town.

www.artelglass.com

English Language Bookshops and Other Interests

Blue – This is a chain of nicer souvenir shops that has everything from good picture books of Prague to better quality T-shirts and postcards, and, yes, art glass. They have locations all over Old Town (Celetná Street, Malé Náměstí and Melantrichova Street) and on Mostecká Street in Malá Strana (on the right as you walk off of the Charles Bridge).

www.bluepraha.cz

Botanicus – these shops sell hand-made soaps, shampoos, oils, etc. and actually grow the ingredients for their products on their own farm in the Czech countryside. Good gifts to take back home – unlike the glass and crystal, most of these products won't break, are small, and can easily be packed in your luggage. The main store is located in Týnský Dvůr just off of Old Town Square, and it was so successful they added another one a few meters across from it.

www.botanicus.cz

Manufaktura – Modeled on the same theme as Dr. Stewart's with more of a Czech flare, including many wonderful handmade Czech wooden toys. Manufaktura has many locations throughout Old Town and Mala Strana (on

Mostecká Street leading to the Charles Bridge). More good gifts to take back home, including beer shampoo.

www.manufaktura.cz

Le Patio – This shop, opened in the early 90s by a Belgian expatriate, was at the time of its founding the only place in town where one could find decent gifts and home décor items. Such was the situation at that time in Prague that on birthdays my friends and I would open one gift after another that had come from Le Patio, and the homes of just about all of my friends in the expat community were decorated with Le Patio items (until they were all decorated with items from Ikea and then progressed from there). Now that there's plenty of choice on the market, Le Patio is still an old favorite. Dušní 8 in Old Town near the Spanish Synagogue (and near No Stress Café, which is decorated with Le Patio furniture and other accessories).

www.lepatiolifestyle.com

Bookshops – There are a few English-language bookshops in Prague, all with very good selections, especially considering their relatively small size. The shops' offerings also include lots of local interest books and works by Czech authors translated into English.

• **Shakespeare & Sons** – located in Malá Strana, this little shop has a very good selection of English language books (as well as a lot of fairly cheap used books in case you need to pick something up for that flight home or a train ride to Berlin!). On Kampa Island near the Charles Bridge and Kampa Park restaurant. U Lužického Semináře 10.

www.shakes.cz

• **The Globe** – This is the oldest English-language bookshop in Prague, featuring a wide range of titles, a cozy atmosphere and not bad food and coffee in the café.

Pštrossova 6.

www.globebookstore.cz

• **Franz Kafka Bookshop** – while not strictly an English-language bookshop, this place has a pretty good selection of books about Prague in English and a really nice art book selection. Its name is a nod to the fact that Franz Kafka's father once had a shop in the ground floor of this very building, the Rococo Kinský Palace, at Old Town Square 12.

Puppets (Marionettes) – Czechs love puppets and their puppet theaters. Many festivals and other events will include puppet shows for children, and there's even a theater in town that regularly puts on the opera "Don Giovanni" with puppets! Consequently, puppets are popular Prague souvenirs. Most souvenir shops and outdoor markets sell puppets of varying quality and size. A few shops sell the more authentic wooden, hand-carved ones. But in the center of town these are dwindling, as they can't support the high rents.

At the time of this update (March 2017) there were a couple of shops left in town: two in the Ungelt (Týnský Dvůr) behind the Týn Church (one next to and one at the opposite end of the courtyard from Botanicus) and two in Malá Strana just under the Charles Bridge (on your right as you come off the bridge on the Malá Strana side) on U Lužického Semináře.

Cuban cigars – as with gelato, if you decide you'd like to smoke a few genuine Cuban cigars while you're in Prague, there are a couple of humidors you can check out: One is the Cigar Club at La Bodeguita del Medio on Kaprova Street (Kaprova 5, near Old Town Square) and the other is La Casa del Habano on Dlouhá Street (Dlouhá 35), which runs off of the other side of Old Town Square. I have no idea what will happen if you try to take them back to the U.S. and the customs agent finds them (though the restrictions may be loosening?). So, I'll leave that up to you. But you can smoke them here with no problem.

www.labodeguitadelmedio.cz
www.lacasadelhabano.cz

Tesco – This is a British department store that can satisfy all of your practical needs (including a grocery store in the basement and a convenience/news section on the ground floor). It recently underwent a major renovation and facelift, and it is now quite appealing. One of the best additions was a Costa Coffee shop (a British imitation of Starbucks) on the ground floor in the rear, in case you need a refreshment break when you hop off the 22 tram on your way back from Malá Strana or Prague Castle. For the summer months, a new terrace restaurant and grill located on the roof offers a different view of this part of Prague.

www.mystores.cz
Tram: 2, 9, 18, 22 to Národní Třída.

Outdoor Markets

Havel's Market (Havelské Tržíště) – One of the city's oldest markets, Havel's Market is located on a site that has served as a market for centuries. When I first moved to Prague, this market comprised mostly fruit and vegetable stands with a few flower sellers thrown in. Now, the fruit and vegetable stands have shrunk to a pitiful few, with rather junkie souvenirs taking over most of the space. However, there are a few decent photographs and paintings for sale (careful – some of the paintings are originals and some are prints), and some of the souvenirs aren't bad either, like the hand-painted Prague-themed bookmarks and refrigerator magnets. So, you might be able to pick up a few small and easy-to-pack gifts for friends here, and there's always a Prague tee-shirt or beer stein to be had. Located near the Estates Theater on Havelská Street at the corner of Melantrichova in Old Town.

Tram: 2, 9, 18, 22 to Národní Třída

Metro: Můstek (green or "A" line and yellow or "B" line)

Old Town Square, Kampa Park (Na Kampě) and **Ovocný Trh** – each of these squares originally served as marketplaces, and on special occasions or during certain seasons, each still does today. Old Town Square more often than not has some kind of market operating (such as an Easter market or a Christmas market, etc.). The quality, authenticity and desirability of the goods on offer vary from not bad or even interesting to kitsch to downright ugly. But the atmosphere can sometimes make up for this.

The food on offer is usually better than the souvenirs and other products. The "Prague Ham" you'll see roasting in open pits is especially good. But be aware that it is served by weight and the server will invariably pile a huge amount of meat on your paper plate and say, "OK?" You'll nod yes and then they'll quickly weigh it and you'll end up paying around $12 for a plate of street food. As I said, the ham is very good, but you can get a full meal with a beer in a pub for that amount of money. So, just be sure to watch how much ham they give you before you agree to have it weighed, at which point, there seems to be no turning back.

Markets are held less often on the Na Kampě square on Kampa Island (next to the Charles Bridge in Malá Strana) and on Ovocný Trh (behind the Estates Theater just off of Old Town square) and they tend to be a bit more interesting and of better quality than the ones on Old Town Square. Around Bastille Day there usually is a very nice French market on Kampa, serving good wines and cheeses and other French delicacies.

In September you'll find wine festivals ("vinobrani," or wine harvest), and in the spring and autumn there are beer festivals around town (usually at Prague Castle or on the embankment of the Vltava just south of Palackého Náměstí).

Farmer's Markets

The locavore trend began to infect Prague about two years ago. What started as one or two farmer's markets that were held only occasionally and then mostly in the warmer months has now turned into a network of markets to be found on almost every square (outside of the touristic center) almost year-round, several days a week. My locavore and fellow foodie friends all agree that the one at Náplavka is the best. It is probably the one you'll be most interested in, as well, as it is held along the picturesque river embankment on Saturday mornings, not too far from the center of town. The Náplavka market has a great atmosphere and food trucks with hot meals in addition to the farm fresh products. You can check the following link for more info on all of Prague's markets.

www.farmarsketrziste.cz/en

Note: as of this update, the city authorities are attempting to move the Náplavka market further out of town. Let's hope not, but I will make an update if it does happen, so check the website before you go.

Shopping Malls

I know – you probably don't want to go to a mall while you're in Prague. But not all malls are created equal, and a few of the malls here have some unique features, so, just in case....

Palladium Shopping Center – This mall is located in a former historical army barracks, and the beautiful façade of the original building was left intact. On the lower floor, you will find excavated Romanesque ruins that were left exposed and incorporated into the building. And finally, the food court in this mall has some pretty good restaurants in addition to the usual fast food suspects. The Mexican restaurant is quite good, as is the Lebanese El Emir. And, of course, the mall has restrooms (all on the uppermost/food court level and on the lowest underground level), free Wi-Fi at the Starbucks downstairs and at the McDonald's upstairs, and ATMs ("bankomat") sprinkled throughout.

Nový Smichov Shopping Center (otherwise known as "Anděl" by locals) – at the Anděl tram and metro station in Smíchov. Like the Palladium, this mall was built on the site of a historical building (a factory in this case), whose rather attractive façade was left in place. The mall is pleasant enough, and has restrooms (only on the upper two levels for which you now have to pay CZK 10), cash machines, a Tesco grocery store, a Marks & Spencer, cinemas and decent cafes (and now two recently-added Starbucks locations). It also has a Česká Spořitelna branch on the ground level that does foreign exchange.

Tax-Free Shopping

Non-EU tourists in Prague are eligible for a refund of the VAT of up to 21% on purchases over CZK 2,000. Look for stores with a "Tax Free Shopping" sign, and be sure to ask the clerk for a tax refund voucher when you make your purchase. You will then have to present this voucher and original receipts to an agent at Prague airport. Look for "Global Blue" at Terminal 1. I believe they are located **before** you go through passport control, but if you can't find them, please be sure to ask before you pass through passport control. At Terminal 2, look for the Travelex office.

Note: Some shops in town offer to refund your credit card for your VAT amount to save you the hassle of having to do it yourself. Basically, this amounts to a scam (or almost) and I would not do it.

www.globalblue.com/destinations/czechrepublic/tax-free-shopping-czech-republic

Notes

_____
_____
_____
_____
_____
_____
_____
_____
_____
_____
_____
_____
_____
_____
_____
_____
_____
_____
_____
_____
_____
_____
_____
_____
_____
_____
_____
_____
_____
_____
_____
_____

6 DON'T MISS

Many of my tour clients come to Prague for only a few (2-3) days. With such a short visit, that means there probably will not be time to see all of the major sites in each of the four main historical areas (Old Town, Malá Strana, the Jewish Quarter and Prague Castle), and I often get asked, "What should I see, X or Y?" So, in case you don't have much time in Prague, I've put together my "Don't Miss" list to help you decide what to put at the top of yours.

My list is what I would personally advise you not to miss if you have time to see them all, or what to choose from if you don't. **Please note that my list also assumes that you will in any case see the sites on Old Town Square (including the Astronomical Clock), as it's the heart of the touristic center of Prague, and the famous Charles Bridge, so these sites are not included here.** This is a list of what to see **in addition** to these "must-sees."

The Jewish Cemetery, the Pinkas Synagogue, and the Old-New Synagogue - In the Jewish Quarter

In order to see these sites, you will have to purchase an

entry ticket that admits you to all of them, with the exception of the Old-New Synagogue, for which you can buy an entry ticket to it alone, if you wish. Of course, the Jewish Quarter is an important and interesting area to visit, but if you don't have time to see the whole quarter (which takes about half a day), I would consider buying a ticket to all the sites anyway and seeking out these three significant locations, especially the very moving Jewish Cemetery. Tickets can be purchased at the Spanish Synagogue on Vězeňská (and your ticket is good for several days, in case you do have more time but don't manage to see all of the sites the first time around).

And, of course, you can see the synagogues from outside without buying a ticket, but not the cemetery. And the most interesting parts of the Pinkas Synagogue are the exhibitions inside. Take the metro to Staroměstská (green or "A" line) or Tram 17 to Právnická Falkulta.

The "Old" Part of St. Vitus Cathedral and Vladislav Hall in the Old Royal Palace – At Prague Castle

As with the Jewish Quarter, Prague Castle takes at least half a day to visit and is definitely worth your time. But if your time is really limited, I would put the "old" part of St. Vitus (the eastern end past the transept, which was begun in the 14th century) and Vladislav Hall at the top of your list.

To enter the Prague Castle sites, you will need to purchase one of two types of tickets: a "short visit" or a "long visit". In my opinion, the "short visit" ticket is sufficient in any case, as it will get you into the majority of the Castle's most significant sites, including the two I mention here.

Note, however, that you can wander around the castle grounds all you like and see its structures from the outside without buying a ticket (in the summertime this is especially nice, as the grounds are open into the evening when it's usually much less crowded). Of course, many of the Castle buildings' interiors are historic as well as stunning, so you will miss a lot by not buying a ticket. However, that's not to say that a walk through the Prague Castle grounds is not worthwhile. Also, at the time of this writing (April 2016), you are allowed to walk **into** St. Vitus Cathedral at the western (newer) entrance without a ticket, but you can only stand in the back and have a look but not walk **around** and see the older, and, frankly, more interesting, eastern end which dates from the 14th century. In order to venture further into the cathedral you will be required to scan your ticket at an electronic gate set up in the aisles. Take tram 18 or the metro to Hradčanská (green or "A" line) or tram 22 to Pražský Hrad, or walk uphill on Nerudova fom the Malá Strana (the hill is fairly steep and long and could prove difficult if you have difficulty with mobility).

St. Nicholas Church, Both Inside and Out – In Malá Strana

Don't miss this 18th-century Baroque masterpiece, especially the over-the-top interior. You've probably never seen anything like it! This church was meant to make a major statement during the Counter-Reformation, and it does. And Mozart played the organ here in 1787. You'll have to pay a small entry fee (around CZK 70), and be sure to pick up a brochure on the ledge of the ticket booth before you present your ticket for entry). Located on the upper half of Malostranské Náměstí (tram 12, 20 or 22 to Malostranské Náměstí).

The Estates Theater (Stavovské Divadlo or Nostitz Theater) – In Old Town

This is a stunning Neo-Classical Jewel. And the Viennese opera scenes in the movie "Amadeus" were filmed inside. But perhaps the most amazing fact about this building is this: the world premiere of the opera Don Giovanni took place here in 1787, with Mozart himself conducting the house orchestra. On Železná Street/Ovocný Trh near Old Town Square.

The Municipal House (Obecní Dům)

This Art Nouveau masterpiece is one of Prague's landmarks. Built in the 1910s as part of the Czech cultural revival that was happening at the time, the Obecní Dům is the result of a collaboration between some of the best Czech architects and artists of the day, including Alfons Mucha. In the 1990s, it underwent a total renovation using the building's original blueprints, right down to the last doorknob. Obecní Dům contains a concert hall, exhibition spaces, a restaurant, an old world (now touristy but still magnificent) coffee house and more. Located on Náměstí Republiky (yellow or "B" metro line; trams 6, 8, 15 and 26 to Náměstí Republiky).

The Powder Tower (Prašná Brána)

This magnificent 15th-century Gothic tower sits on the site where a medieval gate once stood. It also served as a gate to the town of Prague (the part that is now Old Town) and was once used to store gunpowder, which is where it gets is current name. The Powder Tower marks the start of the "royal way" that once was the route that Czech kings took to the castle to be crowned. Juxtaposed to the Obecní Dům, it makes a striking combination of old and (more) new. Located on Náměstí Republiky (yellow or "B" metro line, trams 6, 8, 15 and 26 to Náměstí Republiky).

The Works of Matthias Braun

Nothing says "Prague" to me like the works of Matthias Braun, especially his statues on either side of the two entrances to the Clam-Gallas Palace at Husova Street 20 (near Karlova Street, which leads to the Charles Bridge in Old Town) and his carved eagles guarding the entrance to what is now the Italian embassy at number 20 on Nerudova Street in Malá Strana. And while you're on Nerudova, take a look across the street at the magnificent Moors guarding the doors at Nerudova 5 by Braun's contemporary, F. M. Brokoff (take tram 22 to

Malostranské Náměstí).

The Façade of St. James Church

This marvelous façade was done by Italian master Ottavio Mosto. The interior is quite spectacular, too, and its nave is the second-longest of any church in Prague after St. Vitus' at Prague Castle. St. James also has the best acoustics of any church in Prague, so Sunday mass is a special treat. Located behind the Ungelt on Malá Stupartská in Old Town (yellow or "B" metro line, trams 6, 8, 15 and 26 to Náměstí Republiky).

Notes

_____

_____

_____

_____

_____

_____

_____

_____

_____

_____

_____

_____

_____

_____

_____

_____

_____

_____

_____

_____

7 A FEW OF MY FAVORITE THINGS

This section is intended to be just what the title says – a list of some of my favorite things to do and see in Prague. Some of the places will be listed in your traditional guidebook under historical sites. Others might not be well-known or mentioned at all. But all of them are places or activities I have discovered in my years of living here that I never tire of.

Several gardens are mentioned in this section, but be aware that **all gardens in Prague are closed from November 1st through March 31 each year.** Parks are open year-round, except in cases of extreme weather, like the heavy rains and flooding we had this past spring.

The Royal Castle Gardens at Prague Castle

A walk through these beautiful gardens on a nice spring or summer day is incredibly pleasant. While you're there you can take in the 16th-century Belvedere (Royal Summer Palace) and the views of Prague to the right of it. Also take time to see the "Míčovna" (a sgraffito-covered ball-hall built by one of the Hapsburg rulers for sporting fun) and the ultra-modern orangery by internationally-renowned Czech architect Eva Jiřičná (she also designed Hotel Josef in Old Town, one of Prague's first modern boutique hotels). Take tram 22 to the stop Královský Letohrádek.

Wallenstein Garden (Valdštejnská Zahrada) in Malá Strana (also called Waldstein)

As with the Estates Theater, parts of the film "Amadeus" were shot here. These sumptuous Baroque gardens were built by General Wallenstein in the early part of the 17th century to go with his sumptuous palace. Note the bronze copies of the Adrien de Vries statues (the Swedes took off with the originals during the Thirty Years' War, and they remain in Sweden today), the Sala Terena and the amazing grotto (if you look long enough, you'll discover the fascinating faces of unusual creatures). Take a tram (2, 12, 15, 18, 20 or 22) or green or "A" metro line to Malostranská.

Vrtba Garden (Vrtbovská Zahrada) in Malá Strana

These Italian Baroque sculptured gardens feature works by Baroque master sculptor Matthias Braun. Be sure to walk all the way to the top, stopping at various points during your ascent to turn and look at the changing views of Prague unfolding before you. Don't stop until you've climbed the hidden stairs at the very top of the garden for stunning views of the Castle, St. Nicholas Church and much of Prague. Take tram 12, 20 or 22 to Hellichova.

Kampa Park on Kampa Island

This quiet park in Malá Strana offers a respite from Prague's busy (and at times quite noisy) streets. I especially love the view of the Charles Bridge, the National Theater and the far side of the river embankment when standing at the river's edge near the Kampa Museum. Enter from near the Mala Straná side of the Charles Bridge or from the other end near the tram stop Újezd (trams 9, 12, 15, 20 and 22).

The Tram 22 Ride Between Náměstí Míru and Prague Castle (Pražský Hrad)

Take in the fairytale-like panoramic view of Prague Castle, the Charles Bridge and the Old Town Bridge Tower as this tram crosses the Vltava (Moldau) river. The ride through the winding streets of Malá Strana is also very nice, as is the "serpentine" stretch from the Malostanská stop up to the Royal Summer Palace (Kralovské Letohradek). Near the other end of the 22's route, Náměstí Míru is the architecturally beautiful heart of Vinohrady.

The Tram 18 Ride from Staroměstská to Národní Divadlo

This ride offers stunning views of Prague Castle and the Malá Strana side of the river (the opposite side of the river from the 18's route) and Petřín Hill. Embark at the Staromestská stop headed south or at the Národní Divadlo stop on Národní Třída headed in the direction of the Staroměstská stop.

Tram 17 follows the 18 for part of its route. Headed south from the Staroměstská stop on the 17, continue for two more stops past Národní Divadlo to Palackého Náměstí to see a beautiful row of Art Nouveau apartment buildings and Frank Gehry's "Dancing House" facing the river.

Náměstí Míru and the Vinohrady Neighborhood

Take a walk through this one-time wealthy neighborhood, with its beautifully and elaborately decorated 19th-century apartment buildings. And not only is it beautiful, but Vinohrady is also one of the trendiest areas of Prague these days, especially when it comes to dining. The streets near the square, including Americká (to the right of St. Ludmila's church as you face it) Korunní (behind the church), and Manesova to the left of the church (past Vinhoradská), are especially nice.

The Schwarzenburg Palace at Prague Castle

Part of the National Gallery in Prague, the permanent collection of Bohemian Baroque sculpture on display here includes works by Baroque masters Matthias Braun and Maximilian Brokoff, among others.

www.ngprague.cz/en/objekt-detail/schwarzenberg-palace/

Great Views

There are many places where you can get great views of Prague (and take great photos), especially since Prague is full of towers and is surrounded by hills. Most towers are open for climbing if you have the stamina. Here are some good spots:

• **The Vrtba Garden (listed above)** – as you make your way up this garden, the view constantly changes.

• **The Prague Castle hill** – at either end of the castle complex, you are offered stunning views of the city below, especially the rooftops of Malá Strana. Walk from one end to the other through the Garden on the Ramparts, which offers various lookout points.

• **The Powder Tower (listed in the previous section)** – a walk up this tower will give you great views of the Obecní Dům and surroundings.

• **The St. Nicholas Church tower in Malá Strana** – word has it that the Czech secret police used this tower to spy on the nearby British Embassy in communist times. In any case, the views of Malá Strana from here are magnificent.

• **The tower of the Town Hall of Old Town** – this one has a working elevator to save you the climb to the top. The views of Old Town Square are wonderful.

Notes

8 MUSEUMS AND ART GALLERIES

Like so much of Prague's culture, the art scene here is undergoing a transformation. While great strides have been made in this area since the Berlin Wall fell, I would say that art in Prague still has a way to go in terms of both variety and presentation before it reaches levels comparable to other cities of its size. The city also lacks a definable area where art galleries are concentrated, though I expect one will eventually emerge, perhaps in Holešovice or Karlín. Presently, Michalská Street in Old Town is the only thing that comes close, but unfortunately a true "artists' quarter" does not exist. On the other hand, Prague is really trying, and the entry prices at museums and galleries are a better bargain here than in many other cities. Some of my favorite places to check out are listed below.

The National Gallery in Prague (Národní Galerie v Praze)

The National Gallery is a collection of museums and galleries located throughout Prague. It maintains permanent collections and also hosts temporary exhibitions of painting, sculpture and graphic art, as well as works from the genre of what is known as "new media," by both Czech and international artists. Many of the National Gallery's locations are in former palaces on the Prague Castle (Hradčany) grounds.

As mentioned under "A Few of My Favorite Things," the collection of Bohemian Baroque sculpture at the Schwarzenburg Palace is one of my top picks. Interesting temporary exhibitions are often held in The Prague Castle Riding School, the Salm Palace, and the Waldstein Riding School. Check the National Gallery's website for permanent and current listings.

www.ngprague.cz

The Museum of Decorative Arts

This is one of my favorites, but sadly, in January 2015 it closed for a two-three year renovation. I'm leaving this info anyway in case you come back!

The Museum of Decorative Arts has fun and interesting exhibits of contemporary crafts, applied arts and design. Depending on what the current exhibition is, you might see displays of things like Czech glass and glass-making, fashion, or textiles, etc. A big plus is the fact that many of their exhibitions are fun for kids, like a recent one of Matchbox cars, including an area in which to play with them! Take tram 2, 17 or 18 or the green or "A" metro line to Staroměstská.

www.upm.cz/index.php?language=en

The Lobkowicz Palace Collections

This is undoubtedly one of the best art collections in Prague, and it, too, is one of my favorites. The Lobkowicz Palace also has arguably the best museum shop in Prague. The café is not bad either, and it's a good place to stop for lunch on your tour of Prague Castle. In warmer months, the balcony seating offers beautiful views of Prague from castle hill.

Lobkowicz Palace houses the oldest and largest privately

owned art collection in the Czech Republic, covering more than six centuries of art. One of the highlights of the painting collection is Haymaking (1565) by Pieter Brueghel the Elder. Also on display are the family's collections of silver, porcelain and hunting weapons.

www.lobkowicz.cz/en

The Rudolfinum Gallery

This impressive exhibition space (and adjacent concert hall that is the home of the Czech Philharmonic) is one of Prague's nicer galleries, located in the historic and beautiful Neo-Renaissance Rudolfinum building. Designed as a concert hall and gallery, this space was built in 1884 by the same architects who designed the National Theater. Check their website for current exhibitions. Located across the street from the Museum of Decorative Arts, on Alšovo Nábřeží 12 in Old Town. Take tram 2, 17 or 18 or the green or "A" metro line to Staroměstská.

www.galerierudolfinum.cz/en

DOX Center for Contemporary Art

DOX is the newest and biggest addition to the city's art scene. It was opened five years ago with the aim of putting Prague on the map of contemporary art. DOX has done a good job so far, and the building itself is a former factory converted into a very contemporary space that retains a few of the original details. It also has a quite good gift shop and café. Located at Poupětova 1 in Holešovice, a ten-minute tram ride from the center of town. Take tram 6 or 12 to Ortenovo Náměstí.

www.dox.cz/en

House at the Stone Bell (Dům U Kamenného Zvonu)

This gallery is housed in one of Prague's oldest Gothic

structures, the House at the Stone Bell. The building dates from the 13th century, and its interior contains some of the most beautiful Gothic carving you'll see anywhere. This gallery usually has very good exhibits, so check to see what's on. It's almost worth a visit to an exhibition just to see the stone carving in some of the upper rooms, which you are allowed to photograph for now. Located on Old Town Square.

www.en.ghmp.cz/stone-bell-house/

Czech Photo Gallery (now also called the Nikon Photo Gallery)

This small gallery on Újezd in Malá Strana is a pleasing space with interesting exhibits of photography. And the best part is that admission is free (at least at the time of this writing). Tram: 9, 12, 15, 20, and 22 to Újezd or 12, 15, 20 and 22 to Hellichova.

czechphotogallery.cz

The National Technical Museum

The National Technical Museum in Prague has many fascinating exhibitions on the Czech nation's rather impressive array of technological achievements in everything from transport to printing to astronomy. Take tram 1, 8, 12, 25 or 26 to Letenské Náměstí and walk 3 minutes from there.

www.ntm.cz/en

Notes

9 MUSIC, OPERA AND OTHER PERFORMANCES

Like crystal and fine glass, classical music and opera also define Prague and the Czech Republic. This is a nation of music lovers and music makers (and even the colorful language of which Czechs are so proud is used in an expressive and artistic, even musical, way). The Czech Republic boasts of famous composers (Dvořák, Smetana, Mahler and Martinů), top-rate orchestras (the Czech Philharmonic), lots of opera and talented singers (Dagmar Pecková and Eva Urbanová), and many world-renowned musicians, past and present (Rafael Kubelík, Josef Suk). Prague was also a frequent destination of composers from other lands like Hungarian-born Franz Liszt and Wolfgang Amadeus Mozart, who visited one particular summer house in the suburbs of Prague so often that it is now dedicated to him.

The Prague Spring International Music Festival, (Pražské Jaro), one of the world's best known classical music festivals, is held in May of each year. There are other notable festivals, as well, like the newer Prague Proms, which is held every June-July. Otherwise, concerts in Prague are ubiquitous year-round, and you will be inundated with offers as you tour the city center's streets. Some are better than others. Some are excellent and some are what are known as "tourist" concerts: classical music's greatest hits distilled into an hour. But that doesn't mean they aren't enjoyable or good. The good news is most concerts and opera performances in Prague are of a quite high quality and are cheaper than in the U.S. and other parts of Central and Western Europe. Here are some venues, festivals and ticket sellers to check out:

Orchestras, Theaters and Theater Companies

The Czech Philharmonic and the Prague Symphony – both of these orchestras offer top notch talent and performances.

www.ceskafilharmonie.cz/en
www.fok.cz/en

The National Theater (Národní Divadlo) – the National Theater features opera, drama, and ballet at several venues (the National Theater, the Estates Theater and the State Opera).

www.narodni-divadlo.cz/en

Music Festivals

The Prague Spring International Music Festival – Held in May of each year, this festival has attracted top notch talent and music lovers from all over the world for decades. It also takes place in what is usually one of the nicest months of the year in Prague, and while the festival is on, the whole city is abuzz with concert goers every afternoon and evening, creating a special atmosphere. But note also that many hotels raise their rates during Prague Spring.

www.festival.cz/en

Prague Proms – This is a new festival on the Prague music scene featuring international artists and a mix of musical styles, from classical to jazz, pop to gospel. Prague Proms is held in June and July, and the theme varies every year.

www.pragueproms.cz/en

Concerts Around Town

Concerts around town are held just about everywhere, mainly in churches and in some of Prague's synagogues. (Note that most churches are not heated, so take that into consideration in winter. Those with heating will proudly advertise this fact.) Some good places to look out for are:

St. Nicholas Church in Mala Strana – This church has concerts almost every evening, and some of them are of quite good quality. Stop by to see what they have on while you're in town. The acoustics are pretty good, and the interior is over the top! Located on Malostranské Náměstí.

St. Nicholas in Old Town – Concerts are held here daily. Its organ has a beautiful quality, and you'll be seated under a stunning crystal chandelier made in the glass-making region of northern Bohemia. Located on Old-Town Square.

St. James Church – This church with its incredible façade has a beautiful sounding organ and the best acoustics of any church in Prague. It also has music at its regular mass on Sundays, so if you want music, you could go either for a concert or to worship. Its interior is a good example of Bohemian Baroque. Located on Malá Stupartská in Old Town.

The Spanish Synagogue – Concerts are held regularly at this 19th-century synagogue with a stunning interior in the Moorish style. Located at Vězeňská 1 in Old Town.

Theaters

Prague has many theaters which put on various dramas, comedies and more. But most are in Czech, of course, so this might not be accessible for you. But Prague is also well known for its "black light theaters," where performances take place in a darkened space with a black background and illuminating costumes. Usually, these performances are without dialogue, which means they can be enjoyed by everyone. You will see flyers and other ads for black light theaters around town, but one of the best is the Image Theater.

www.imagetheatre.cz/en

The Czechs are also known for their much loved puppet or marionette theaters. Some even put on "Don Giovanni," Prague's most popular opera. The best is probably the National Marionette Theater at Žatecká Street 1 in Old Town.

www.mozart.cz

Ticket Vendors

TicketPro – Conveniently located on Wenceslas Square, TicketPro has tickets to most events in Prague.

www.ticketpro.cz/jnp/hudba/klasicka-hudba-operni-arie

Bohemia Ticket – Online, you can purchase tickets with a credit card, but the last time I bought tickets in the Bohemia Ticket office they accepted only cash! That was several years ago, though, so I am not sure if that is still the case.

www.bohemiaticket.cz/WBS/ang/

Cinemas

I know – as with malls, you probably don't plan on visiting a cinema while in Prague, either. But since this book is about my favorite – and unique – Prague attractions, a few are worth mentioning in my view.

When I arrived in Prague, cinemas were the old-fashioned kind: one showroom with old (very hard) wooden seats like those found in old school auditoriums. By the end of a two-hour film, you were ready to get out of those seats, but, on the other hand, tickets were CZK 16, which at that time was about 50¢. The first "multiplex" in Prague opened in the mid-nineties, and besides having more than one film to choose from (and more comfortable seats), it also had popcorn. Next the cinemas at Slovanský Dům opened with the most modern features and the most comfortable seats I had ever seen anywhere at the time.

That trend continues today: The things that are new in Prague now are all from the same, current time period – i.e., the very recent past. The reason is quite simple: during 40 years of communism, nothing was updated here, not to mention the fact that anything "trendy" or "cool" or luxurious would have been frowned upon and banned. So everything that is truly new in Prague is **really** new, up-to-date and state-of-the-art. Prague's cinemas, interestingly, now make some in the U.S. seem outdated by comparison.

Now practically every shopping center in Prague has multiplexes, and 3-D is the new thing (4-D, too). But with all this "development," the old-fashioned cinemas had difficulty surviving (though many of them held on for a long time). **A few of them, however, transformed themselves into art house cinemas** with unique programs, features and attractions, as well as first-run Hollywood films at a cheaper price than the big chain multiplexes (if you're willing to wait a week or two). Two of the most popular are listed below:

Kino Světozor – located in the Tesla Pasáž on Vodickova Street near Wenceslas Square. This centrally located cinema screens many Czech, Hollywood and foreign films, as well as film festivals and live broadcasts from New York's Metropolitan Opera, the National Theater in London and the Bolshoi Ballet. Its regular program features a series called "Documentary Mondays," showcasing documentaries on a wide range of topics. And often a film's director will stop by for a discussion of his or her work, as was the case recently when the director of "Far From Heaven," Todd Haynes, answered viewer's questions after a screening of his film.

Kino Světozor also has a nice bar with beer and a decent South African wine by the glass that you can take into the cinema with you. Check their program at:
www.kinosvetozor.cz/en

Kino Aero – located on Biskupcova Street in the hip-cool-grungy neighborhood of Žižkov. This is one of the coolest places in town, as is the crowd that hangs out there. Like Světozor, Kino Aero has an interesting mix of films and live Met and other broadcasts. Two of its special programs are "Aero na Slepo" ("Blind Date") and Film Jukebox.

Aero's "Blind Date" night works like this: you have no idea what film will be screened, so you enter the screening hall "blind" – and for free. If you don't like the film, you can leave within the first 30 minutes and pay nothing. If you like the film and choose to stay, you pay at the end.

Film Jukebox is a monthly screening of whichever film that Aero's fans voted for on the cinema's website during the previous month. This has brought some classic films back to the big screen, like "Scarface" and "JFK."

Besides the cinema itself, Aero has a sleek modern bar that is quite a surprise after you make your way to the premises through a nondescript alleyway off of a small street. They serve cheap beer, Czech and decent French wine, and bar food. It's non-smoking until 9:00 PM, and in the summer you can enjoy your beer or glass of wine in the courtyard. And, of course, you can take your beer or wine to the movie, too!

www.kinoaero.cz/en

Notes

_____

_____

_____

_____

_____

_____

_____

_____

_____

_____

_____

_____

_____

_____

_____

_____

_____

_____

_____

_____

_____

_____

_____

_____

_____

_____

_____

_____

10 PRAGUE FOR KIDS

This chapter was added in September 2013 when I first published a paperback version. In the earlier (Kindle editions) I hadn't included any information on what to do with kids in Prague mainly because I don't have kids, so I really felt that I didn't have a clue in this area. Nor have I had many tour clients visit with small children (though I have had several teenagers). But of course many of my Prague friends have kids, and a few friends from the U.S. have visited with their children recently, so I decided that perhaps by now I do have a few suggestions that might be helpful.

The Prague Zoo (Zoo Praha)

The first time I visited Prague's zoo in the 1990s, it was one of the most depressing things I had ever experienced. Without going into details, suffice it to say that I decided that I didn't want to ever visit there again, and I didn't – until a few years ago when a friend was planning to take her little girl to the zoo and invited me to go along.

In the years since my first visit, I had heard that the zoo was undergoing a big renovation and upgrade, including the addition of a botanical garden, yet I still didn't expect much. Well, you can guess that I'm going to say that I was pleasantly surprised. The place was quite improved, very interactive, very interesting and user-friendly.

Further testament was supplied during a recent visit by an American friend who had lived here for a year in the roaring 90s. In 2013, she returned for the first time with her two young daughters, eager to show them the city she loved and had told them so much about. Her older daughter, who is very tech-savvy as kids are these days, had done her own research on Prague in anticipation of their trip and found out that Prague has a zoo. She was hellbent on seeing it, as was her little sister, who had been clued in by the older one.

When my friend and her girls finally got to Prague, I spent a day with them, and my friend confided, with a weary look, "They want to go to the zoo. I don't know about you, but I remember that when I went there, it was just awful. I don't want to go." I told her that I knew what she meant and that I had felt exactly the same way when I first visited it, but that the zoo really is much better now. In the end, they went, and my friend happily reported, "The zoo was great! Put it in your book for people who come here with kids."

So, there you have it. That's my Prague Zoo story – quite a transformation. I have heard good reports from others as well. Of course, if you're not a zoo person or are opposed to the concept of zoos, it's not for you, even with the upgrades. Located at U Trojského Zámku 3, Prague 7.

www.zoopraha.cz/en

Bus: 112 from the Holešovice metro station (red or "C" line) to the stop Botanická Zahrada Troja

The National Technical Museum

I mentioned this in a Chapter 8, but repost it here, as their exhibits are also quite interesting for children. See their website for more details.

www.ntm.cz/en

Tram: 1, 8, 12, 25 or 26 to Letenské Náměstí and walk 3 minutes from there.

Hard Rock Café

Teenagers, especially, like this place, but younger kids do as well. Prague's Hard Rock is much like the others, though the building housing it (the neo-Renaissance V.J. Rott building) is quite extraordinary and historic. The burgers aren't bad, either, and supposedly it's Europe's largest Hard Rock. Located on beautiful Malé Náměstí, just off of Old Town Square.

Phone: 224-229-529
www.hardrock.com/locations/cafes3

The John Lennon Wall

Your teenager will also enjoy seeing the John Lennon Wall and the chance to leave his or her mark on an historic site. This is the only place in Prague where graffiti is legal (though, unfortunately, that doesn't stop misguided youths from leaving it everywhere else). Younger children might enjoy all the colors here, too. Located in Malá Strana on Velkopřevorské Náměstí across from the French Embassy, near the Malá Strana end of the Charles Bridge. **Tip: Bring a Sharpie!**

Black Light Theater

This form of theater apparently originated in Asia but has become a specialty of Prague, which is full of them. "Black lighting" (UV light) and fluorescent costumes combine to create intricate visual illusions. A good one is the Image Theater (mentioned previously under "Music, Opera and

Other Performances).”

Paddle Boats

In the summertime, this is a fun thing for kids and adults to do (I suppose children below a certain age must be accompanied by an adult). There are a couple of locations where you can rent them on the Vltava riverbank near the Legii Bridge (Most Legií), by the National Theater.

IMAX Theater

The Flora shopping mall in Vinohrady contains this well-known brand of 3-D cinema. But be aware that most films for children shown here are dubbed in Czech rather than being shown in their original language with Czech subtitles. Inquire about this before you buy your ticket. Occasionally, the cinema in Slovanský Dům will show children's films in the original language.

www.cinemacity.cz/en/imax
Metro: Flora (green or “A” line)
www.cinemacity.cz/en/SlovanskyDum
Metro: Můstek (green or “A” line or yellow or “B” line)

Dino Park

This might be a stretch, but local kids like this theme park. It is located way out in the suburbs at the Galerie Harfa shopping center. Take the yellow or “B” metro line to Českomoravská.

www.praha.dinopark.cz/en

Notes

11 DAY TRIPS

If you're going to be in Prague for more than 3 days or so, you should consider making a day trip to one or more of the many interesting and historic places outside of Prague. Due to its rich history in the middle of Europe, the Czech Republic has many towns and castles whose beauty and historic importance make them worth visiting.

All of the destinations listed below can be reached via specialty tour companies that sell tickets for minibus excursions at various locations throughout the city (most are located on Na Příkopě, near Obecní Dům). Some hotels also offer excursions or a private car with a driver. Some destinations are easily reached by train. Others, like Český Krumlov, unfortunately, are not. I also offer private guided tours of Kutná Hora. It is one of my favorite destinations. Here's a short list of my top picks.

In the Czech Republic

Karlštejn Castle – Built in the 14th century by King Charles IV as a place of safe-keeping for reliquaries and the crown jewels, this fairytale-like castle rises high on a hill near the Berounka River not far from Prague. The heart of the castle is the Chapel of the Holy Cross, with walls covered by semi-precious stones. Access to this part of the castle is limited due to the need to maintain certain atmospheric conditions, so check listings; however, the exterior and other interior spaces are regularly available for tours. Karlštejn is about a 30-40 minute car or train ride from Prague (trains leave regularly from the main train station, Hlavní Nádraží).

Nelahozeves Castle – Just 35 kilometers north of Prague, this Renaissance castle belongs to the Lobkowicz family and features one of the finest private art collections in Europe. Across the street from the castle, you can see the birthplace of Czech composer Antonín Dvořák. A train ride from Masarykovo Nádraží to Nelahozeves takes about 30 minutes. Enter only with private guided tours booked in advance.

Konopiště Castle – Undoubtedly the most famous owner of the Konopiště Castle over its many centuries of existence (since the 14th) was the archduke Frantisek (Franz) Ferdinand d'Este, a successor to the Austro-Hungarian throne whose assassination in Sarajevo in 1914 became a pretext of World War I. Konopiště is about 30 minutes from Prague by car.

Kutná Hora – This medieval mining town has some of the most beautiful Gothic architecture in all of Bohemia thanks to the riches bestowed on it through its silver mines beginning in the 13th century. The Church of St. Barbora, with its three naves and five aisles, is one of the most beautiful and interesting Gothic structures in Europe. The town also offers stunning views from its hillside walkways, as well as other magnificent buildings such as the Italian Court and the Stone House. Travel time to Kutná Hora is an hour by train and usually about 90 minutes by car, depending on traffic. As mentioned above, I also offer private guided tours of Kutná Hora, including the ossuary ("bone church") and the Cistercian cathedral in the nearby village of Sedlec. See "Contact."

Ceský Krumlov – Words can't do justice to this fairytale-like medieval town. From the Rumplestiltskin tower to quaint art galleries and the cafes along the rushing Vltava (Moldau) river, one must simply visit Ceský Krumlov in order to experience and soak up its special atmosphere. It's a three-hour drive from Prague, so it's best to stay overnight, but it's doable in a day if you must.

Beyond the Border

Dresden – Day trips are also possible to Dresden by train or car. I prefer the train option, as the highway between Prague and Dresden was never completed on the Czech side (the government ran out of money), and the result is not only a slower trip than the train, but also a confusing one on which the traveler almost always loses a lot of time navigating one particularly confusing and poorly-marked interchange that invariably sends one ether: 1) on a loop that you will repeat at least once, or 2) **off** of the section of the highway that actually **was** completed and back to the original old two-lane road that will certainly put you behind a slow, exhaust-spewing truck most of the way back to Prague. And don't count on your GPS having this particular stretch of road updated, either.

The train, by comparison (be sure to take an "EC" or "IC" train), takes about two hours and 15 minutes and traverses a particularly beautiful section of the Elbe River valley along the limestone cliffs of what is known as "Czech-Switzerland" (or "Saxon-Switzerland" if you're on the German side of the border). This picturesque train ride is one of my favorites anywhere.

The EC/IC trains are international trains, which generally means that they are clean, comfortable, and air-conditioned, and they are mostly on time (and usually direct to most major destinations, which is very important when travelling by train through the Czech Republic, where local trains with lots of stops and changes take much longer and are sometimes unreliable). The EC trains from Prague to Dresden leave every two hours beginning in the early morning and continuing until early evening in each direction. In the evening, the frequency is less often than two hours, so check the schedule.

Also, the EC/IC train from Prague to Dresden continues all the way to Berlin and Hamburg if you want to continue your journey, or to Budapest in the other direction from Prague. It is recommended that you buy a seat reservation ("místenka") for this train, especially if you are travelling in the summer from Prague to Berlin, and even more especially if you are traveling on a Friday – every backpacking college student who has come to Prague will be headed to Berlin for the weekend on the Friday trains.

Vienna – Technically speaking, you can go to Vienna and back in a day. But given the time it takes to travel there by car or train (about 5 hours), I wouldn't recommend it. Unless you want to get up **really** early and/or get back **really** late, you will end up with only about five hours in which to see Vienna.

That means you would walk around for a couple of hours and see (from the outside) a few main sites and buildings in the center of town, sit down in one of the famous (and wonderful) cafes for a delicious coffee and cake, and then head back to your bus or train. Vienna deserves more than that. But, as I said, it's doable in a day if you don't have more time and simply must **"see"** Vienna (you won't be able to do much more than "see" it). If you can, stay over one or two nights.

As with the trains to Dresden, go for an "EC" or "IC" train. These will normally be direct, clean and on-time, and the trip to Vienna takes just under 5 hours one-way. Surprisingly (to me at least, given the distance and the high price of gas here), many of the tour companies that offer trips to the above-mentioned destinations also offer day trips to Vienna. The train is slightly cheaper.

In case you do go to Vienna, Café Demel, which once was the chocolatier to the Emperor, is my favorite Viennese café. They've been making chocolate here every morning for 500 years. And you can watch the continuation of this ritual through the kitchen's glass wall. And be sure to have a schnitzel at Figlmuller if you have time.

www.demel.at/en
www.figlmueller.at/en

If you are coming to Prague and plan on taking train trips to other destinations, I can help you research timetables and purchase your tickets for you under my **"Concierge Services."** Contact me via email at: krysti.brice@seznam.cz or see my website for more information:

www.exclusivepraguetours.com/concierge.

Notes

12 HOTELS AND APARTMENTS

In earlier editions of this book, I hadn't included any information on hotels for many reasons. Mainly, I don't have personal experience with hotels in Prague – because I live here, I've never stayed in one. And since one of my conditions in writing this book was that everything recommended had to be something I personally have experienced, know and like, hotels didn't make the grade for inclusion. Furthermore, most of my tour clients already have a hotel booked by the time they contact me, and since I'm not a travel agent, I just didn't have a lot of contact with hotels.

Occasionally, however, clients have asked me about a particular hotel they were considering, and while I was able to tell them whether it was in a good location in relation to the historic city center or public transport, etc., being able to say something about the rooms, service, and, especially, rates was another matter.

But I have always made it a point to ask my clients how they like wherever they are staying, and sometimes they are very enthusiastic about their accommodation and have shared with me about how great their hotel is, or what a great deal they got, etc., (or how bad something is). And in the past few years, it just so happened that a lot of clients asked me to give an opinion on various alternatives they were considering or to recommend a hotel. In response, I did some research and, combining it with the feedback I've gotten from clients, I now feel comfortable putting together some recommendations. In addition, I now have an exclusive arrangement with a luxury hotel, The Mark, whereby I can offer a discounted rate if you book through me.

So, I've included a list of hotels for you to check out in various categories: Luxury, Mid-Range and Budget. Please note that the categories I've used, as with my restaurant price categories, are my designations based on the range here in Prague and the hotels I'm most familiar with. They are not official designations of any sort, and, of course, each hotel has its own official "star" designation, up to five stars.

Luxury

The Grand Mark Luxury Hotel Prague – As mentioned above, I have an exclusive agreement with The Mark under which I can offer discounted rates. The Mark, a member of the Leading Hotels of the World, has a comparable level of luxury to the Four Seasons but at lower prices. The staff and service are very good and the hotel's location in Old Town is great. The rooms have been completely renovated in a modern and luxuriously-appointed style. They are also quite spacious for a European hotel in an older building.

Check my website where you can find more information on The Grand Mark and photos of its rooms, suites and other facilities, or contact me if you would like me to check rates for you (**krysti.brice@seznam.cz**). My special rates also include the hotel's fabulous breakfast buffet free (a $25 value per day per person) and automatic upgrades to a suite if available on arrival).

www.exclusivepraguetours.com/hotels

The Four Seasons – The name "Four Seasons" speaks for itself. The Prague version is very luxurious, is in a fantastic location (if there's not a flood happening!) and can offer stunning views of Prague Castle. And it is very expensive.

www.fourseasons.com/prague

Augustine – One of the newest additions to Prague's luxury hotel category, the Augustine is located in a former monastery in Mala Strana. The restaurant is supposed to be excellent (I've not yet tried it), and the service is good (based on my interactions with staff when meeting tour clients there). Clients who have stayed there also reported that they liked the hotel very much, enjoyed their stay, and that the service was very good.

www.theaugustine.com

The Mandarin Oriental – Also located in Mala Strana, this hotel is a very popular one, for tourists and for locals holding events and meetings. Like the Augustine, it is situated in a former monastery and boasts a very modern and luxurious spa, a good (and expensive) restaurant and a very good bar (deemed a "bar with a big ego" in a recent survey). The Mandarin is expensive but deals are available if you can find them. The rooms are luxuriously appointed.

www.mandarinoriental.com/prague

Mid-Range

Hotel Paříž (Hotel Paris) – This hotel, located next to the Obecní Dům and Powder Tower in Old Town, is oozing with Old World charm inside and out (at least when it comes to style and architecture – I'm not sure if the service is Old World, too). This is one of Prague's most beautiful and famous hotels. The exterior is a stunning 19th-century amalgam of "neo-" name-your-architectural-style. The interior of the ground floor and common spaces is one of the most beautiful Art Nouveau interiors around, thoroughly preserved down to the furniture and fixtures. The rooms have been elevated from their communist drab. (I'm not sure if they have air-conditioning though). This place was made famous in Bohumil Hrabal's novel "I Served the King of England." Several clients have stayed here and liked it a lot.

www.hotel-paris.cz/en

Hotel K+K Central – This hotel is Art Nouveau outside and beautiful high-tech modern inside with a good breakfast. It's also in a very good location with regard to sightseeing and public transport, located on the same street as The Mark and Best Western Hybernská near Náměstí Republiky. K+K Central occupies one of Prague's most beautiful and historic Art Nouveau buildings and has been completely reconstructed on the inside. I've had many clients stay here who all give it high marks. Note that if you try K+K be sure to go for K+K **Central** (it's a chain so there are other K+K hotels in Prague, but this one is in the best location).

www.kkhotels.com/en/hotels/prague/k-k-hotel-central/welcome/

Hotel Josef – This ultra-modern hotel can boast that it is the work of internationally-renowned Czech émigré architect Eva Jiřiřná. It was Prague's first "boutique" hotel and caused quite a stir when it opened. Its Old Town location is great, and they serve a good breakfast. Clients and friends who have stayed here recommend it. The rates are reasonable.

www.hoteljosef.com

Hilton and Marriott – I know, you don't want to go to Prague and stay in an American hotel… you want Old World charm or something more local. But I include these because of their good location – and in case you have any rewards points you can use.

Note that Prague has two Hiltons – one in Old Town on V Celnici 7 (called, appropriately, Hilton Old Town) and the other on the river, which is in a less desirable (though not bad) location a few tram stops from Old Town and in a cubic structure that was part of the last gasp (thankfully) of communist construction in Prague. So, I'm speaking of the Old Town Hilton here. It is right across the street from the Marriott (originally it was actually purpose-built by Marriott as a Renaissance Hotel, which is a chain owned by Marriott, at around the same time Marriott built its namesake across the street). Yes, when you walk into the rooms of either of these hotels, you might think you are in any Marriott in the Midwest, right down to the bathroom fixtures and American beds with lots of pillows (which, in my view, is a plus).

But as I said, the location of both of these hotels is ideal for sightseeing (near Obecní Dům and the Powder Tower), shopping (next to the Palladium shopping mall) and transport (next to the Náměstí Republiky metro and tram stations, around the corner from the Masarykovo regional train station, and one tram stop from Prague's main train station, Hlavní Nadraží). They are also fairly easily accessed by car and have underground parking. And the Marriott has the "usual" amenities (gym, etc.).

The Hilton is a bit more upscale in terms of service, and its lobby, restaurant, and reception area have been stylishly redecorated with a fireplace for warming up after sightseeing on a cold winter day. But the small size of the rooms reflects the fact that it was purpose-built as a Renaissance.

www.marriott.com/hotels/travel/prgdt-prague-marriott-hotel/
www.hiltonpragueoldtown.com

Budget

Sheraton Charles Square – While it's a 10-minute walk (or one tram stop) away from Old Town, this hotel is definitely worth considering. I have had tour clients stay here who recommend it, (one of them very highly) and I have attended business functions here. The young manager is working hard to make this one of Prague's stand-out locations, and in pursuit of that goal he is striving to provide top-notch customer service and value for money.

The last tour client of mine who stayed at the Sheraton raved about the service, perks (like a free and substantial warm buffet in the evenings) and the great room rate he got online (which included breakfast). Even though it's not in the touristic center, the Sheraton is right next to a major tram stop and metro station (Karlovo Náměstí) in an attractive 19th-century building that has been completely renovated with modern facilities.

www.sheratonprague.com

Best Western Hotel Pav – This basic hotel, also a 10-minute walk from the major sites, is located in the vicinity of the Sheraton and right next to the famous U Fleků brewery and restaurant. Clients who have stayed here liked it just fine. For longer stays or stays with kids, it is easier on the wallet than hotels located in the touristic center.

www.hotel-pav.cz/en

Apartments

The Hunger Wall – I have friends who come to Prague from the U.S. several times a year and always stay here. I have seen the apartments so I can recommend this place. The Hunger Wall has quite a local feel as it was originally a beautiful old (late 19th-century) apartment building that's now been converted into this residence hotel. The Hunger Wall is located in a stylish neighborhood close to Kampa Park and the National Theater on the Malá Strana side of the river.

http://hunger-wall.prague-rentals.com/

Prague City Apartments – Some tour clients and the same friends who usually stay at the Hunger wall have also used this service. And some of my Prague friends regularly use Prague City Apartments for their visitors, as well. I have seen the Karoliny Světlé and Břehova locations, and both were very nice, very modern, and completely renovated, with maid service included.

Just be aware that this company has lots of locations, and I have heard complaints that their Karlova Street location was "too noisy." Karlova Street is the main drag in Old Town leading to the Charles Bridge, and therefore it is packed with tourists year-round, day and night. My advice is to check locations when booking and try to stay away from Old Town Square and Karlova Street.

www.prague-city-apartments.cz

Airbnb – Of course, Arbnb has hit Prague in a big way, with apartments for rent all over the city, in and out of the historical center – and with the usual accompanying local opposition to the firm's impact on housing availability and pricing, real or not. I've had a few clients use the service, and some of the flats I saw were spectacular. Most clients have been satisfied with what they got here, so if you're a fan, give it a try.

www.airbnb.com

Notes

_____
_____
_____
_____
_____
_____
_____
_____
_____
_____
_____
_____
_____
_____
_____
_____
_____
_____
_____
_____
_____
_____
_____
_____
_____
_____
_____
_____
_____

13 RECOMMENDED READING AND DVDs

Many books have been written about Prague, by Czechs and foreigners alike. And the Czech Republic has produced many internationally-renowned writers, including its former dissident president, the playwright Václav Havel. The influential Franz Kafka was from here - born not too far from Old Town Square and buried in a Prague cemetery.

Prague also has a thriving film industry, and many of the current movies and television commercials you see in the U.S. and elsewhere were filmed here. But you might not be aware that even during the dark days of communism, many Hollywood and other films were made here. One is the movie "Amadeus," starring Tom Hulce and F. Murray Abraham, which was filmed almost entirely in Prague. The film's Czech director, Milos Forman, needed to re-create 18th-century Vienna, and in Prague he found a place that required almost no staging, inside and out.

The wonderful thing about "Amadeus" (besides the fact

that it is a wonderful movie), is that you get to see how Prague looked under communism and how it still looked when I arrived in 1992, seemingly untouched for decades, with everything faded to an almost uniform beige. You can also see, even in the decaying fringes of buildings, the timeless and unchanging beauty of this city. If you have not seen this movie – or even if you have – I strongly suggest that you see it (or see it again) before you come to Prague! (And my tours include many of the locations featured in the film.)

Viewers with sharp eyes will know that much of Barbara Streisand's "Yentl" was filmed in the Czech Republic, with a beautiful aerial shot of her horse-drawn carriage traveling across the Charles Bridge near the end of the movie. The quaint medieval town of Český Krumlov is featured as well.

To enhance your experience of Prague, I've put together a list of recommended books that I think you might find interesting to read before your trip or during your travels. They are all available from Amazon.com and other booksellers. On my website, you can find links to all of these titles that will take you directly to Amazon.com, as well as a complete list of my recommendations:

www.exclusivepraguetours.com/books--dvds

Here's a sampling from my list:

"For the Love of Prague" by Gene Dietch – This is a very interesting account of life under communism as told by perhaps the only American who lived here through most of it. It's a fascinating story of love and the harsh reality of life in the Czech Republic from the 1960s until the Velvet Revolution.

"Open Letters" by Vaclav Havel – This collection of writings belongs to the world's "literature of conscience." These letters by Havel, the playwright-turned-dissident who would become president, includes his famous essay, "The Power of the Powerless" and more.

"The Trial" by Franz Kafka – This work by Kafka eerily points to things to come, as an ordinary citizen is accused of a crime he didn't commit and yet cannot prove his innocence or free himself, as he gets sucked into "the system."

"Where She Came From" by Helen Epstein – I love this fascinating account of one woman's (and one family's) struggle during the Holocaust and ultimate survival. In her book, Epstien, who was born here but grew up in the U.S., delves not only into the history of her family, but also into the history of the Jewish population of the Czech lands. I learned more about Czech Jewish life and history from this book than from any other source.

"Prague Winter" by Madeleine Albright – Albright, who was born in Prague, tells of the dark time of the Nazi invasion and occupation of Czechoslovakia, the sad fate of Czech Jews (including her own family members) and her family's war years spent in London in this, her latest book.

"The Good Soldier Svejk" by Jaroslav Hašek – A Penguin classic by Czech writer and anarchist Jaroslav Hašek who uses satire to depict the futility of war.

"The Unbearable Lightness of Being" by Milan Kundera – This is perhaps the greatest work of Czech-born author Milan Kundera, who is considered by many to be one of the world's great writers. It was also made into a feature film.

"Life Under a Cruel Star" by Heda Margolius Kovaly – A wonderful memoir, this book tells of one woman's survival of the horrors of the Holocaust, the hope and promise many saw in communism, and the gradual creep of a different kind of horror as communism's totalitarian grip took hold in former Czechoslovakia. Eventually, Margolius Kovaly's husband, who was a true believer in communism after WWII, becomes one of the victims of the system he helps to create, as he is one of the eleven who were arrested, tried and convicted in the Slanský "show" trials. This is a fascinating yet tragic tale.

"Amadeus" (DVD) – This Oscar-winning film by Czech director Milos Forman (who also directed "One Flew Over the Cuckoo's Nest) is not only a great film but was also shot almost entirely in Prague. Prague's timeless city streets form the backdrop that should be 18th-century Vienna, and the film also offers a glimpse of how Prague's old city center looked in the last days of communism.

"Yentl" (DVD) – I watched this film for the first time and after having lived here for many years, and I was pleasantly surprised when I began to recognize the backgrounds as familiar places in then-Czechoslovakia. Featured prominently are the city of Český Krumlov and an aerial shot of Barbara Streisand's horse-drawn carriage crossing the Charles Bridge near the end of the movie.

14 PRACTICAL MATTERS

Pickpockets

Prague is a very safe city in terms of violent crime. However, it does have very good pickpockets, and they target tourists. So be VERY careful of your wallets, etc., especially on trams, in the metro and in groups or crowded areas, which is just about all major historical sites. They also occasionally target "touristy" locations, like the cafes mentioned previously. So, just be aware of your personal belongings while sitting down for a coffee. And be especially careful on trams 9 and 22 (which goes up to Prague Castle) and at the Muzeum metro station (which is quite crowded with packed escalators and small passageways in some places).

The packed space in front of the Astronomical Clock on Old Town Square just before each hour and the small, crowded space in front of St. Vitus Cathedral at Prague Castle are also targeted areas. This is not meant to frighten you or put you off. It's just to make you careful so that you don't have a big downer on your trip.

Language

To say that the Czech language is very difficult is, well, a major understatement. And Czechs themselves will tell you, almost with glee, about how difficult their language is – so difficult, in fact, that even Czechs struggle to learn it and get it right. When I first arrived, I remember being told by many people about the common need to hire speech therapists to help children learn to pronounce certain Czech letters, especially the terribly difficult "ř," and that some Czechs are never able pronounce it correctly, if at all (former President and writer Václav Havel being one of them). **Fortunately, most people in hotels, shops and restaurants speak varying levels of English these days, so language shouldn't be a problem on your visit.**

Most restaurants have English versions of their menus, or they will have one menu with each item listed in Czech and several other languages, including English. Just be aware that often the quality of the translation is quite bad, so in some cases the English is almost of no help at all – or is downright unappetizing. And sometimes it's good for a laugh! **Here's a heads-up on a common translation mistake:** "Pečené koleno" is usually translated incorrectly as "pork **knuckle**." This puts a lot of people off as they think they would be ordering pigs' feet. It is actually roasted pork **knee**, served with mustard and grated fresh horseradish, and it is delicious.

For taxis and asking for directions, you might want to have your destination/address written down, or point to the street name on a map, as non-Czech speakers can have difficulty with the pronunciation of Czech words and names, resulting in your not being understood. I've also put a handy vocabulary guide at the end of this chapter so that you'll be equipped with some useful words and menu terms.

The "Prague Post"

This is the best English language newspaper in town, with entertainment and restaurant listings included. Alas, the print version just recently bit the dust, but there is a limited online edition at **www.praguepost.com**.

Taxis

If you hail a cab on the street, they might try to rip you off. Therefore, I would recommend using one of the reliable taxi dispatching services. The best is AAA Taxi. Their numbers are: 603-33-11-33 or 729-33-11-33 or 233-11-33-11. If you are in a restaurant and want to take a taxi from there, you can ask the restaurant staff to call for you. Just tell them to call Triple A or "Ačko" (pronounced "Ahchko"). It's possible your restaurant might use a different taxi service. Usually the taxi companies that restaurants use are OK (Profi Taxi is one example).

If you call AAA, you'll get either an operator or, if they are busy, a recording alternating between Czech and English telling you what number you are in the line/queue of callers. Be patient – even if your number is quite high, the line moves quickly. When you get an operator, she will ask you for your name and address (where you are or where you want the taxi to pick you up), so have the address or restaurant name ready before you call. She might also ask you where you are going. Then she will tell you to hold while they look for the car nearest you. When they have located the car, an automated voice will tell you the vehicle number and approximately how long it will take the car to arrive. Normally, the drivers are waiting throughout the city, so **it is rare to wait more than 5 minutes**. Then, look for a taxi outside your location with an "AAA" sticker on it. Look for the car number also, to be sure you don't take someone else's cab. When you get in, the driver will ask for your name, thereby ensuring that you are not getting someone else's cab and that he/she has the correct passenger.

It's also possible to reserve taxis in advance, say, if you want a taxi to pick you up to take you to the airport for your return flight home. Your hotel concierge or reception desk will be glad to order a taxi for you. Just tell them to call AAA.

Also, in contrast to the U.S. and many other places, it is common here for a passenger to occupy the front passenger seat next to the driver. You don't have to, but don't be surprised if the driver offers you this seat, especially if you are the only passenger. Taxis at the airport, however, have started to catch on that this is not what people from most other countries are used to, so I've noticed that they have started to automatically open only the rear passenger door for customers.

Uber (www.uber.com/en-CZ/) is also operating in the Czech Republic now, and many of my tour clients prefer to use this service as there is no need for cash and not much of a language issue. **Liftago** (www.liftago.com/) is another app-based taxi service that will offer you many different drivers/cars/prices to choose from.

Note: Most Czech drivers are normally quite aggressive on the road – unfortunately, it's part of the national psyche. So expect your cab ride from the airport (or wherever) to make you feel more like you've landed at Euro Disney and taken your first adventurous ride rather than having taken a normal cab ride in Central Europe.

Transport from the Airport

Taxis from the airport – After much political wrangling, AAA finally got an official taxi dispatcher and stand at both of the main terminals of the Prague airport about five years ago. Unfortunately, last year their contract was up, and a new tender was held. AAA did not win, and two other companies now share the monopoly on taxi service at Prague airport. When I returned from my most recent Christmas/New Year's visit in January 2017, I was surprised and disappointed to see that AAA service was no more at the airport and that in its place was FIX taxi service and one other company. FIX, as the name is maybe meant to imply, is the taxi service that routinely gives unsuspecting customers (i.e., foreigners) the "fix" at Prague's main train station. Left with little choice when I arrived in January, I gave them a try (after asking for a price estimate up front). While the actual price of the journey to my home was within the estimate, it was quite a bit more than AAA. But thankfully it wasn't a total a total rip-off, either, and the driver did use the meter. So, for the next five years, we're stuck with these two taxi companies at the airport. I only wish the city would enforce some rules on FIX at the train station.

When you exit baggage claim, look for a bright yellow booth with "AAA Taxi" on it. The dispatcher will direct you to waiting taxis just outside. A ride to the city center will cost between CZK 550-700 (approximately US$23-30 at current exchange rates) depending on where your accommodation is located. Note that the maximum number of passengers that a regular taxi sedan can legally take is 4. So, if you have more people in your party, speak to the dispatcher who can order a minivan (hopefully). If not you'll have to take multiple taxis. AAA from the airport accepts Czech crowns and Euros

Airport shuttles – CEDAZ offers a minivan service that will take passengers to hotels in the city center, or to designated central locations like Náměsti Republiky. It is cheaper than a taxi or car, but the drawback is that you might spend literally hours driving around Prague in slow, jammed traffic while each passenger is taken to his/her hotel (plus you have to wait for the van to fill up before it leaves the airport).

Public transport from the airport – There is also a public transport information booth at each of the arrivals halls at the airport where you can get a map and buy bus, tram and metro tickets. Bus 119 goes to the Nádraží Veleslavín metro station (end of the green or "A" metro line) where you can change to the metro (subway) or to trams which will take you to the city center or other metro/tram lines. It is very cheap (CZK 32, or about US$1.50).

The only drawbacks are that the bus is usually standing room only and takes a while to get to the metro. Also, at the Nádraží Veleslavín metro station, you will have to carry your bags down stairs, as there is no escalator to the first underground level. Elevators, if they happen to be installed in a particular metro station, are iffy as to whether they are working. So, depending on how many bags you have or how heavy they are – and how mobile you are – the public transport route for getting to/from the airport might not be the best option. But for getting around Prague, public transport is generally wonderful (just watch out for pickpockets).

Another city bus that runs to and from the airport is number 100. It will take you to the Zličín metro station, which is at the end of the yellow or "B" metro line. The same precautions for Nádraží Veleslavín apply.

Transport from Train Stations

Unfortunately, **Prague train stations remain good locales for dishonest taxi drivers to rip off unsuspecting tourists**. I still hear the bad stories from my tour clients and others. **Here's the bottom line: all of Prague's train stations are located within the city, either in the center or close to it. So, unless your hotel is way out in the suburbs, a taxi ride from any train station to where you are going should not cost more than CZK 250 at the upper end.** And if you arrive at the main train station (Hlavní Nádraží), it is quite likely that your hotel will be so close that your ride should cost only about CZK 100 (or about US$4). However, I have heard of people being charged – or at least quoted – CZK 1,000 or more. It should never cost that much if you are staying anywhere in Prague!

Currently, there are no official AAA (or other) taxi stands at train stations. So I usually call AAA when I arrive to have a taxi come and pick me up (unless I don't have a lot of luggage and am planning to use public transport). Almost every time, the dispatcher sends me to a different place to meet my car. It seems that taxi stands were not originally included in the stations' designs, so the pickup and drop-off areas are constantly changing as the service roads and tram access points go through their incessant upgrades.

As I write this (April 2016), Prague's main train station is undergoing a major renovation (which is welcome, since the interior was a dreary communist gray, and the exterior is a crumbling Art Nouveau beauty). One hopes that the benefits of having an official dispatcher like the one at the airport will be noted and applied here.

But until then, **my best advice, if you don't have a phone on which you can call AAA, is to negotiate with a taxi driver upfront**. You will probably still be overcharged a bit, but if you refuse at the start to pay more than, say, CZK 300, you'll probably be able to get the driver to agree to this or even less. It helps if you know where your hotel is on a map relative to the station, since it **is** possible that the **real** (honest) fare will be more than CZK 250 if the driver has to travel through winding streets and heavy traffic to reach your hotel if it is not located right around the corner from the station. So, he might actually be telling the truth when he says it will cost CZK 300 or so. But don't pay more than CZK 500. You can almost get to the airport for that, which is a 40 minute drive from the center.

Public transport from all of Prague's train stations, on the other hand, is excellent. All of them are located on top of metro stations, usually with the same names as the train stations to which they are connected, and all are well-connected to trams stopping just outside of them. They all also offer ample opportunity to buy tram and metro tickets – at newsstands or at the ticket machines in the metro stations (but you will need coins for the machines). So, if you don't have a lot of bags, this is a good option. However, keep in mind that to use the metro you will have to go up or down stairs with your bags at some point.

Public Transport

This is really the best way to get around Prague, other than with your feet! The tram, metro (subway) and bus options are convenient, safe, quick and cheap. The trams are, for me, not only the most convenient way to get around (they wind all through the tiny streets of Old Town and Malá Strana), but they are also a great way to do sightseeing. And you can just about set your watch by them and their timetables! Many of the older red and tan trams built in the early 1960s are still in use, adding to Prague's uniquely quaint atmosphere (and in the winter, their seats are heated!).

The number 22 tram from the Národní Třída stop (just outside Tesco) up to Prague Castle has the most beautiful route in the city, taking you across the Vltava river with breathtaking views of the Charles Bridge and Prague Castle, through Malá Strana by St. Nicholas church and up the beautiful serpentine route to the castle (stop: Pražský Hrad). Going in the other direction (back downhill to town from the Castle), take it all the way to Náměsti Míru for a look at one of Prague's most beautiful 19th century squares and a walk around the stylish and trendy neighborhood of Vinohrady. **Here's a tip: For the best views, sit on the right side of the tram when riding up to the castle (and when crossing the river going in the same direction) and sit on the left side going in the other direction (back down to town)!**

A 60-minute tram-metro-bus ticket will cost you CZK 32; a 30-minute ticket costs CZK 24. These can be bought in metro stations and at, unfortunately, only very few tram stops (you'll need coins for the ticket machines, which have a button on them marked "Language" or "English"). After selecting your language, press the button next to the type of ticket you want, and press it as many times as the number of tickets you want. So, for example, if you want two CZK 32 tickets, press the button next to that ticket type two times. The machines are kind of slow, so be patient. As you press the buttons, a running total of the amount of money you need to insert appears at the top. After you have stopped pressing, the coin slot will open and you deposit one coin at a time – it will open and close for each coin! As I said, it is slow. Once you have deposited the full amount, the tickets will be printed one at a time and will drop down into the slot at the bottom. The machines are also finicky – they frequently refuse new and certain other coins – so be patient and persistent, and have extra coins on hand if possible!

If you can't locate a machine or don't have coins, transport tickets are usually available at newsstands ("tabák") where you can just ask the salesperson for tram tickets, or "jízdenky" (pronounced "yeez-den-kee"). You'll have to specify whether you want the CZK24 or CZK32 ticket. Your hotel concierge or reception might also sell single-use tickets and maybe even longer-duration passes. But usually longer-duration (such as 3-day) passes must be bought from the ticket machines or at the ticket window in certain metro stations (Můstek, IP Pavlova). A few newsstands have the passes, but you'll have to ask.

When you enter a metro station or get onto a tram, look for the small yellow boxes with a slot in them. Simply insert your ticket into the slot and wait for it to be stamped with the time, date and number of the tram or name of the metro station where you've entered. **Be sure to stamp it only once, even if you change trams or change from bus to tram or metro, etc.** The time stamp "activates" your ticket and starts the clock running for the appropriate time duration of the ticket you've purchased, and you can use it for tram, bus and metro, even on the same ticket, for as long as it's valid.

Keep your ticket with you and handy for your entire journey. You never know when an inspector will come along to check to see if you've got a valid ticket. And you won't see them coming – on trams they are dressed in plainclothes and will look like ordinary passengers until they jump up from their seats – **after** the doors have closed – and whip out a badge and ask to see your ticket. **Warning: they always go for the tourists first!** And, yes, they will recognize you as a tourist. The fines can be hefty, too.

In metro stations, ticket inspectors wear uniforms, but they are strategically hidden from view until you've passed the point of no return (or exit).

Though the 3-day and 1-day passes might be more convenient, they actually are not necessarily cost effective after the most recent fare adjustments. So before you opt for a longer-term pass, think about how often you are likely to hop on a tram or metro during your day and see whether it might actually be cheaper using single-journey tickets. You'll find that when in the center of Prague, you'll probably walk to more places than you might expect because: a) the center is quite small and things are closer than you realize, and b) in much of the Old Town and Malá Strana, there is no public transport that runs **through** it (rather, it runs in a ring around it), so sometimes you have no choice but to walk (or call a taxi if you have problems with mobility). Also, when crossing from Old Town to Malá Strana, you will probably want to cross the Charles Bridge, which is only possible on foot. So it is quite likely that you will use a tram or metro only once or twice per day, whereas you need to use a three-day pass about 5 times a day to get your money's worth.

Until recently, if you got stuck in Malá Strana without a tram ticket, there was only one place to buy them: the "tabák" (newsstand) tucked around the corner from Starbucks on Malostranské Náměstí (when facing Starbucks, go around it to the right and to the back). However, a coin-operated ticket box has now been installed at the Malostranské Náměstí tram stop (on the same side of the stop as Starbucks).

At the bottom is a button where you can select English as the operating language of the machine and follow the instructions I gave previously. However, if you don't have enough coins or if the machine is out of order, hopefully the "tabák" tucked near the back of the parking lot you're facing will be open (and will still carry the paper tickets – it did the last time I was there).

Trains

You can check Czech and international train schedules at the link below. There's an option at the bottom right of the page where you can chose English.

www.jizdnirady.idnes.cz/vlaky/spojeni/

You can buy train tickets at Prague's main train station (Hlavní Nádraží) or at most of the other train stations such as Nádraží Holešovice in the Holešovice neighborhood (both of these stations are on the "C" or red metro line). You can also purchase tickets at Čedok (the Czech travel agency left over from the state-owned Communist days) on Nekázanka near Náměstí Republiky (the official address they list is Na Příkopě 18, but the ticket office is actually around the corner).

If you're traveling round-trip, say from Prague to Dresden and back, you can get a discount on the fare if you purchase your ticket at least three days ahead of time (round-trip only). If you travel with a group of at least six, you can get a significant discount off the price, possibly even on one-way tickets. There should also be discounts for children, students and seniors (with proper ID). Ask the ticket agent about discounts **before** you buy your tickets. As I mentioned previously, this is the land of Kafka, and no one tells you anything unless you ask (and be aware that even then, there's a big chance you're being told what you want to hear, so double check!). And be sure your ID is acceptable and meets the requirements for a discounted ticket – the age and other requirements are strictly enforced.

You can also purchase tickets online on the Czech Railways website. This option offers substantial discounts on a limited number of tickets (that tend to sell out quickly). But, be careful if you use this option, as **the restrictions are many, complex, and strictly enforced**. For example, you will have to enter your exact name and passport number when purchasing the ticket online. This information will be printed on your ticket, and **you** must use that ticket (you can't give it to anyone else) and the info on the ticket will have to match your travel documents exactly. The same is true for anyone traveling with you on such a ticket (the information on their ticket must match their documents exactly). Also, you must buy a ticket for a certain train on a certain date at a certain time, and you must take **that** train. So, you can't go to Dresden for the day and decide to take a later train back if you're having a good time or running late. You must take the train for which you've purchased a ticket. Otherwise, you will owe the full fair (in addition to what you've already paid for your online ticket).

And if you are traveling with others, all the people in your party who have purchased the ticket for a particular train must all take that train together both ways or your ticket will not be valid and you will owe the full fare. So, if your travel companion gets ill, say, and decides to stay in Prague while you take off for your train trip, you'll lose your online discount advantage. So, for fewer hassles, buy a regular ticket at a train station or at Čedok (three days ahead of time if you can). Or, of course, you can take your chances with an online ticket!

Weather/Clothing/Shoes

Like they say about the English, the Czechs talk a lot about the weather – because it changes all the time. Rain is always a possibility, especially in the spring and autumn. While you'll need clothes for warm weather in the summer, you should also bring things you can layer, like a light jacket or sweater, as it can get cooler at night. And we can even get unexpected cool periods in summer requiring the heating to be turned on, so **check the forecast before you travel**. Winters are cold – sometimes very cold – and you can usually expect snow (while you can't necessarily expect cleared sidewalks). Rain gear is a must in Prague; be sure to be prepared for walking around in wet weather (and snow in the winter), just in case.

Comfortable walking shoes are a must. Not only will you probably be doing a lot of walking, but most of the streets and sidewalks in the old parts of the city are cobbled. So, good, comfortable walking shoes will make a BIG difference.

Money

The currency used here is the Czech crown ("koruna" in Czech), and at the time of this writing the exchange rate is around CZK 25 to US$1 (in the "good ol' days," you got 40 crowns for your dollar!) and approximately CZK 27 to euro 1. **Be sure to check exchange rates before your trip.**

You can, of course, exchange money at many of the exchange offices located throughout the city or at a bank. **But, if you choose to go to an exchange office, be sure to read the fine print before you change anything** – often the advertised rate is applicable only for **very** large amounts of money, much more than you would likely need on a holiday. Lesser amounts are changed at very disadvantageous rates. **Actually, most of these exchange offices really amount to a scam.** So, I prefer exchanging money at a bank.

Many shops and restaurants accept euros, and the rates they give are not bad. But check the rate with your server or clerk before using this option. If you're not headed to the Eurozone after you leave Prague, you might want to get rid of your euros this way, especially if otherwise you would have to exchange more money for crowns anyway.

If someone approaches you on the street and asks if you want to "change money," do not do it. It's a scam, and you will walk away with worthless Belorussian or some other currency hidden behind a CZK 100 note (worth about $4).

You can also use your normal bank, debit or credit cards at ATMs ("bankomat" in Czech). Just be aware that the fee for each withdrawal at a bankomat is US$5, plus a percentage of the amount withdrawn, so be careful about the frequency of withdrawals and associated fees.

ATMs

ATMs ("bankomat" in Czech) offer an "English" option on the first screen under languages. On their default screens, most offer a maximum withdrawal of CZK 4,000 (about US$160). However, you may opt out of selecting a default amount by hitting the "Other Amount" option. This way you can withdraw more than the default amount in order to avoid multiple withdrawals. Just be sure you've done a quick conversion into U.S. dollars of the Czech amount you want to withdraw so that you don't inadvertently exceed your card's limit and get your card blocked by your bank.

Many ATMs now offer two new options when making withdrawals with a bank card from a foreign bank: "Accept with Conversion" or "Accept without Conversion." I use "without," as the option "with" seems to use an even worse exchange rate.

Here are a few ATM/bankomat locations to save you time looking, as they're not so easy to find in the old city center:

- **Palladium Shopping Center** on Náměsti Republiky (several machines near the front and side entrances and on the lower level). Take the yellow or "B" metro line or trams 6, 8, 15 and 26 to Náměstí Republiky,

- **IP Pavlova** and **Náměsti Republiky** metro stations,

- **Česká Spořitelna** bank at the corner of Rytířská and Melantrichova Streets,

- **Mostecká Street** and **Malostranské Náměstí** in Malá Strana.

And here is a list of some bank branches where you can change money:

- **Česká Spořitelna** bank branches: at the corner of Rytířská and Melantrichova Streets in Old Town, on Mostecká Street in Malá Strana and in the Anděl shopping mall at the Anděl metro and tram stop,

- **ČSOB** bank branch on Náměsti Republiky.

If you plan to change money at a bank, note that you will not find bank branches open on the weekends, not even on a Saturday morning. Also, many bank branches close during lunchtime or early (1:00 or 4:00 PM) on certain days of the week. Check the hours posted outside or try to get there in the morning. **In general, when you change money at a bank or exchange office, you will need to have your passport with you.**

Note: If the bank is closed and you only want to use an ATM, you should be able to access some branch's ATMs by swiping your bankcard.

If you have large bills (which in Prague means a CZK 1,000 note or larger) and try to buy something for a much smaller amount, expect to have trouble changing it

(especially with taxis). You will almost surely be met with "Nemáte menší?" ("Don't you have anything smaller?"), and some places will flat out refuse to accept your money or sell you anything! Many shops and vendors seem to be fine with losing a sale over this. So, if you get large bills at a cash machine (and cash machines will almost **always** give you large bills!), try to change them as soon as you can, like when paying for a more pricey item or a meal for several people. And hold onto your small bills and coins for use at cafes or markets or for buying tram tickets or post cards, etc.

If you do change money at a bank, ask them for smaller bills and maybe they will accommodate your request. Thankfully, some ATMs now offer an option where you can choose the denomination of your bills, but CZK 1,000 is usually the smallest on offer if you withdraw a larger amount (which you'll want to do in order to have fewer withdrawals and therefore fewer $5 withdrawal fees as mentioned before, and because CZK 1,000 is only about $40!).

Here's a tip: If you're stuck with large bills and can't seem to get change, go to McDonald's or Starbucks and buy something small – just to get change. They are the only places that are almost certain not to give you a hard time – they won't even ask you if you have something smaller – what service! They will simply change it for you. McDonald's requires you to buy something, though. Starbucks might do it without a purchase if you ask nicely, but I can't guarantee that. Note that in nicer restaurants, paying with larger bills shouldn't be a problem.

Credit Cards

Most restaurants and shops accept major credit cards (Visa, MasterCard, Diners; however, American Express is not as widely accepted as in the US). Using credit cards is more convenient than dealing with ATMs and cash. Therefore, I would use this option where possible. But be aware that most credit cards issued in the U.S. will charge a "foreign transaction fee" on purchases you make abroad.

In general, I would advise you to be sure to check the amount being charged before signing or entering your PIN for a credit card transaction. There have been incidents of credit card fraud in the past. While I have heard of this happening, I personally have never had any problem with using a credit card in Prague. I would advise paying cash in the junkier souvenir shops, to be on the safe side. But at places listed in this book, it is OK.

Restrooms

Though there is still room for improvement when it comes to restrooms, the situation has improved a LOT since the days when I arrived and you had to pay a little old lady for your tiny scrap of "toilet paper" (if you could call it that) and had to suffer the humiliation of her monitoring how long you took and the state in which you left the (fairly atrocious in those days) facilities. There were also long lines at many restrooms.

For the most part, that has changed, though in many places you will have to pay (CZK 5 or 10 – another reason to save your coins). However, the new requirement of paying a small fee usually means that: the facilities will be clean, (more or less – remember that clean is a relative term); and you should have (enough) toilet paper (and will get to decide for yourself how much you need!).

All restaurants and pubs will have a restroom, and, unless you are out in the countryside somewhere, they will be clean and modern – very modern, in fact: many of Prague's restaurants and other new public places have some of the trendiest, most modern and interesting restroom facilities you'll see anywhere! Part of the reason is that they are almost all new (just like the cinemas I mentioned). Everything has been renovated in the years since the communist regime fell, making up for 40 years of stagnation, a rather unnatural phenomenon in the development of any place. So, ironically, this nation that was frozen in time and very behind in many things, and also quite poor, now has some of the trendiest, most up-to-date and modern objects around.

If you're out and about and need facilities, you can always go to any restaurant and ask (nicely) if you can use the restrooms, and you will usually be told yes (I don't think I've ever been turned down), though at some of the big tourist traps, like the café at the Obecní Dům, you might be, or either treated not very nicely. All shopping malls have restrooms, though they are almost always annoyingly located on the upper floors (strategically positioned so that you will have to pass by and view the display windows of a lot of the shops in order to reach them).

And, of course, there is good ol' McDonald's for restrooms. You will have to pay, but they are usually clean and have toilet paper. You will also get a receipt for your restroom fee that you can then use toward your food bill, should you have anything – **after** you've used the restroom. If, however, you pay for your food first, you're out of luck – you can't then get your restroom fee back, nor show your food receipt for entry into the restroom.

Starbucks is also a welcome addition in this area, though they have equipped most of their restroom doors with locks requiring a numerical code to open them. The code is printed at the bottom of your receipt (if you've bought anything). But if you haven't ordered anything and ask for the code, they will give it to you. Or, you can search the tables for someone's discarded receipt or, as a last resort, stand outside the restroom door until someone comes out. But that could take a while depending on how busy (or not) your chosen Starbucks location is.

Some metro stations and all train stations have restrooms. You will have to pay CZK 5-10 at all of these, but they, too, are (nowadays) clean and have toilet paper (at the main train station, they now charge a whopping CZK 20 – to pay for their upgraded facilities, I suppose, and to take advantage of the station's heavy tourist traffic). But be aware that at many of these facilities there is usually only one "communal" role of toilet paper placed at or near the entry, within eyeshot of the attendant. You will have to take what you estimate you will need into the stall, the point of no return.

I guess this system is left over from the communist days when people would steal toilet paper – when I moved here, most toilet paper was padlocked to its holders and soap was tied to the wall in a net, even in workplaces (no kidding). The other peculiarity that is left over in these places is the extremely pungent and unusual smell of the industrial strength cleaner they use to clean them. Try not to let it get to you and assume it means the place is extra clean.

In general, especially for the ladies: carry a pack of tissues around with you, just in case, and always check to see if the seat is clean and dry before you sit on it. I'll say no more. Finally, restrooms are usually marked with "WC," "Toalety," or "Záchod," or "Muži" (men), "Ženy" (women), "Dámy" (ladies) and "Páni" (gentlemen – which is really confusing since another word for lady is "paní" with an accent on the "i" instead of on the "a"!).

Pharmacies

Pharmacies ("Lékárna") are marked with a green cross symbol used throughout so much of Europe. They will be able to satisfy most of your over-the-counter medication needs, including vitamins and band-aides ("náplast"). If you need something like Advil, it's best to ask for the name of the drug/medication (for example, "ibuprofen") rather than the brand name (like "Advil"). Pharmacies are not so easy to find

in Old Town, however. You'll have
shopping malls (Anděl shopping m?
In the center, the only pharmacies th
Max on Národní (across from My/'
Street in Old Town, and another
Street and Wenceslas Square.

There is also a 24-hour pharmacy on one corner c
Míru (at Belgická 37). If you go there late at night and it look.
closed, go to the window on the side and ring the bell.
Someone will appear to help you.

Note that there are many shops around Prague called
"drogerie" (DM Drogerie is a popular one). While the name
seems to imply that they have medications ("drogy" which
means "drugs"), they do not. These shops will carry
everything that, say, a CVS in the U.S. will carry (like shampoo,
maybe some vitamins, cosmetics) **except** drugs. If you need
any kind of medication, you will have to go to a proper
pharmacy (lékárna). This monopoly that pharmacies enjoy
dates all the way back to the middle ages, when guilds
controlled the practice of their craft in their particular towns.
In the Czech Republic (and perhaps in many European
countries), pharmacies still control their "guild."

Basic Czech Words

Everyone agrees that the Czech language is very difficult
(just ask the Czechs themselves). But here are a few useful
words and phrases for you to try:

Thank you: Děkují
Thanks: Díky
Please: Prosím
Good day/hello: Dobrý den
Good evening: Dobrý večer
Good night: Dobrou noc
Goodbye: Na shledanou

Hello or goodbye (informal): Ahoj (same as English Ahoy)
Yes: Ano
No: Ne
Water: Voda
Beer: Pivo
Wine: Víno
White wine: Bílé víno
Red wine: Červené víno
Beef: Hovězí
Pork: Vepřové
Chicken: Kuře
Breakfast: Snídaně
Lunch: Oběd
Dinner: Večeře
Bakery: Pekárna
Pastry shop: Cukrárna
Coffee Shop: Kavárna
Grocery store: Potraviny
Pharmacy: Lékárna

Have a fun and safe trip!

15 CONTACT

Thank you for purchasing my book! I hope you find it helpful. If you're interested in a private tour, please email me at: **krysti.brice@seznam.cz** or contact me through my website at: **www.exclusivepraguetours.com**. And if you're on Facebook, I would love it if you would "Like" my page: **www.facebook.com/ExclusivePragueTours**.

I also offer travel advice and assistance for your stay in Prague. If you want concert information, train tickets or restaurant reservations, I can do all that for you, saving you time and energy that you would spend surfing the web. More details on these and other services can be found on my website: **www.exclusivepraguetours.com/concierge**

And I've recently published a Prague restaurant guide. It gives a much more thorough account of Prague's "food revolution." Find it on Amazon.com or on my website.

Thanks!

PHOTOGRAPHS

(All photographs by the author, including the cover)

The 15th-century "Powder Tower" – This famous tower stands on the site of an old medieval gate. It gets its name from the fact that gun powder was once stored there. Its Gothic design is modeled on the Charles Bridge Old Town tower.

Baroque Statues by Adrien de Vries – The magnificent work of Dutch Baroque sculptor Adrien de Vries can be found in the sumptuous Waldstein Gardens, dating from the 17th century.

The Obecní Dům (Municipal House) – This 20th century Art Nouveau masterpiece is a Prague landmark.

Rašínovo Nábřeží – If you have time, take a walk along Prague's riverbank (above), especially on the Old Town side south of the National Theater. And take time also to taste the delights of Angelato (below).

Old Town Square – The Kinsky Palace (above, left) and House at the Stone Bell and the Tyn Church (below).

MAPS

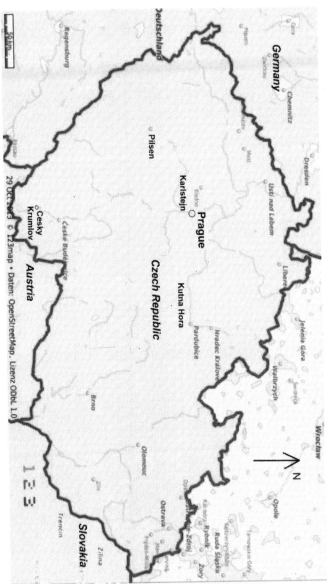

Map of the Czech Republic - ©2013 OpenStreetMap.org

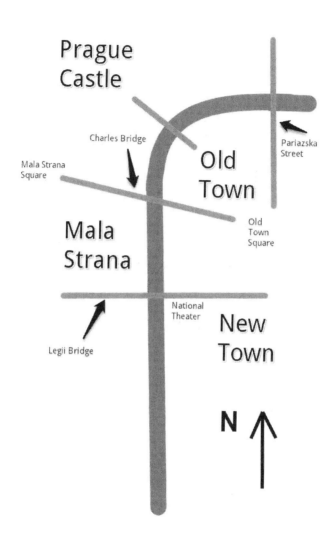

General Overview of Prague

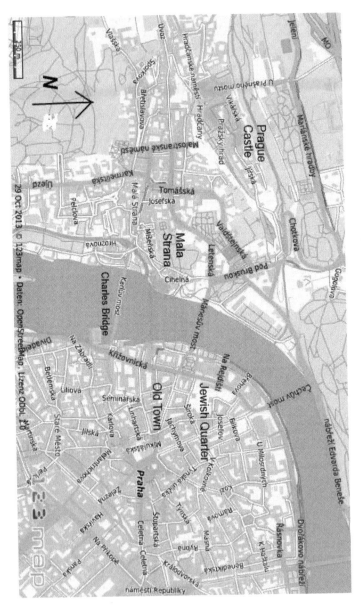

Detailed Map of Prague – ©2013 OpenStreetMap.org

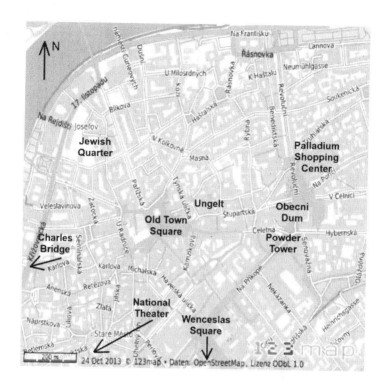

Map of Old Town - ©2013 OpenStreetMap.org

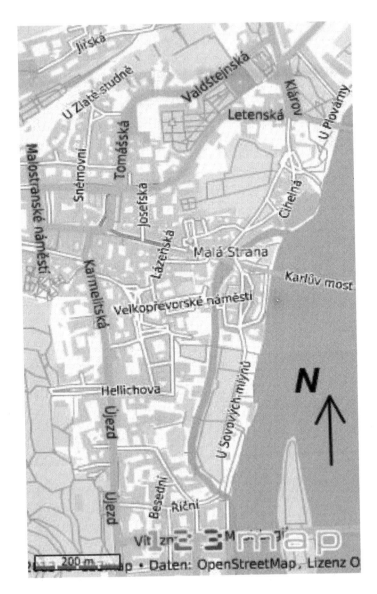

Map of Malá Strana - ©2013 OpenStreetMap.org

ABOUT THE AUTHOR

Krysti Brice, a native of Macon, Georgia, and a graduate of New York University, is a former CPA and investment banker who began her career at Deloitte in New York City. In 1992, she moved to Prague where she continued her work at Deloitte as an adviser to the Ministry of Privatization. While in Prague, she joined the World Bank and was based in both Prague and Washington, DC. After three years in Washington, she returned to Prague in 2000, where she now works as an author, mentor and guide to the city.

Made in the USA
Lexington, KY
20 March 2018